HOW TO SOLVE
CHESS
PROBLEMS

By KENNETH S. HOWARD

SECOND REVISED EDITION

DOVER PUBLICATIONS, INC.
NEW YORK

Published in Canada by General Publishing Company, Ltd., 30 Lesmill Road, Don Mills, Toronto, Ontario.
Published in the United Kingdom by Constable and Company, Ltd., 10 Orange Street, London WC 2.

This Dover edition, first published in 1961, is a corrected and revised version of the work first published by David McKay Company in 1945.

Standard Book Number: 486-20748-X

Library of Congress Catalog Card Number: 61-1978

Manufactured in the United States of America
Dover Publications, Inc.
180 Varick Street
New York, N. Y. 10014

Preface to the Dover Edition

IN this second edition a number of typographical errors have been rectified, some statements corrected, and three problems replaced with other compositions because the previous positions were found to have been closely anticipated by other composers.

East Orange, New Jersey
October, 1960

K. S. H.

Preface

THIS book is intended primarily for the average solver of chess problems; particularly for the one who would like to learn some definite procedures which will enable him to solve with greater certainty and rapidity. For those who have never solved problems, or have done so only occasionally, there is a preliminary elemental section, which may be skipped by more experienced solvers.

Expert solvers vary their methods according to the type of problem on which they are working and in this book no one line of procedure is advocated for use in all instances. The author believes that if a solver is sufficiently familiar with different types of approach, he will choose the one best adapted for each individual problem and soon become able to solve more adroitly and with greater enjoyment. So suggestions are given on solving based on the general construction of the problem, on apparent constructive weaknesses, and on thematic content. In many instances it is shown how the solution may be deduced directly from an analysis of the probable purposes of the various men employed.

The one hundred twelve illustrative problems in *Section Two* are all by United States composers. They have been selected from problems either contributed to or reproduced in the *American Chess Bulletin* from 1935, during which time the author has edited the problem department of that magazine. So, irrespective of the text, the problems form a collection representative of the best modern work of American composers. Naturally the composers who have contributed most regularly to the *Bulletin* have a proportionately larger representation in the selection.

With each diagram, in addition to the name of the composer, there is also given the name of the magazine or newspaper in which the problem first appeared and the date of its publication. A "V" (*version*) before the name of the periodical indicates that, since its first publication, the problem has been revised either to correct some flaw or to improve the setting.

In connection with discussions of the problems, the more commonly employed problemistic terms are explained, and when first mentioned such terms are italicized. The reader can readily find the meaning of any of these terms by consulting the index and turning to the page on which the term is first used. Those who may wish a more detailed explanation of terms and themes are referred to the author's treatise, *The Enjoyment of Chess Problems*.

KENNETH S. HOWARD

East Orange, New Jersey
May, 1945

HOW TO SOLVE
CHESS PROBLEMS

Section One

THIS preliminary section is designed for readers who may have had little or no experience in solving chess problems. No further knowledge of chess is required than that of the movements of the men and the rules of play.

A chess problem is a position arranged to illustrate an interesting chess idea, which frequently is based on some particular characteristics of the various men employed. It is given as a position in which one side can mate in a stipulated number of moves; the majority of problems composed today leading to mate either in two or three moves. Although a chess problem is not primarily constructed as a puzzle, it is a meritorious feature to have the solution difficult to discover.

For the sake of uniformity white invariably is supposed to move first and to mate black. So the stipulation usually reads, "White to play and mate in two moves," or "White to play and mate in three moves." Sometimes it is abbreviated to "Mate in two," or "Mate in three."

The first move of the problem is the *key*. Although any legitimate move may be employed by the composer, it is desirable to have the key an unlikely appearing move, or at least one that does not seemingly strengthen white's position. For this reason the ideal key is exactly the opposite kind of move that a player would select in a game. There is no rule that the key may not be a check or the capture of a piece, but the composer avoids a key of this kind because it would be an aggressive move.

1

In fact there are only two conventions that must be rigidly observed in composing a chess problem. The first convention is that the position must be one which could have been reached in actual play. If this requirement is met, there is no ban on the most unnatural or artificial arrangement of the men, although skillful composers usually try to avoid crowded positions as much as possible.

The second convention is that there must be only one first move, or key, that will lead to mate in the stipulated number of moves. If white has a choice of two, or more, first moves the problem is said to be *unsound* and is valueless. Such a problem would not be published intentionally by a composer or a chess column editor, although solvers often find that published problems do have unintended second solutions.

Careful composers also observe a third convention, which is to use no pieces in the initial position that must have come from pawn promotions. It is unobjectionable, however, to have promotions of pawns occur during the course of the solution, just as they might take place in a game. Problems are even composed especially to feature pawn promotions.

In this volume the notation employed is a form of the *algebraic,* which is commonly used in books on problems because it is more concise and exact than the English notation.

In the algebraic notation the locations and moves of the men always are read from the white side of the board, or the lower side of the diagram. From the lower side the files are designated "a" to "h" from left to right, and the ranks are numbered "1" to "8." Thus white's queen's rook's square is "a1" and black's king's rook's square is "h8."

The same letters are used to denote the men as in the English notation, with the exception of S (German

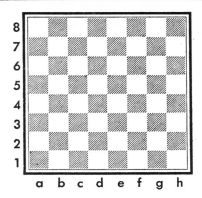

Springer) for knight. 0 – 0 is employed for Castles KR, and 0 – 0 – 0 for Castles QR.

The moves that in English notation would be written: 1 P – Q4, P – Q4; 2 P – QB4, P – K3; 3 QKt – B3, KKt – B3; 4 B – Kt5, QKt – Q2, would appear in the notation used in this book as: 1 Pd4, Pd5; 2 Pc4, Pe6; 3 Sc3, Sf6; 4 Bg5, Sb8 – d7.

The solver will find that the algebraic notation not only is easy to learn, but that it also avoids the ambiguities and confusion which often result from the use of the English notation, in which the solver must count the ranks from one side of the board for white moves and from the opposite side of the board for black moves.

For example, a problem solution written in English notation might run: 1 P – QB4, RxPB5, if there were more than one white pawn that the black rook could capture. Thus the pawn that white moved to his queen's bishop's *fourth* would be captured by black on his queen's bishop's *fifth*. In the form of algebraic notation used in this book there would be no possibility of misunderstanding this play, since it would be written 1 Pc4, RxPc4.

The solver, who wishes to acquire any real degree of solving skill, should, from the very first, practice solving directly from the diagram, rather than by setting the position on a board.

In deciding on a move, when playing chess, the player is not permitted to move the men but is obliged to visualize what may occur if he makes a certain move. Often in a game he has to "look" several moves ahead. This same procedure should be followed in solving problems, and if the solver is only going to move men in his "mind's eye," he will find, with a little practice, that it is easier to do so when looking at a diagrammed position than when the same position is actually set on a board.

Furthermore, when the solver has learned to solve from the diagram, he will also appreciate being able to study problems at many times and in various places where a board and men are not available, or where even a pocket board may not be convenient to use.

*

A

KENNETH S. HOWARD
Chess Review
December, 1935

White mates in two moves

The first problem to be examined illustrates several points. To begin with, note that the black queen is pinned by the white bishop. Problemists employ the word *pinning* in a more restricted sense than it is used by players. In a game a man frequently is said to be pinned by a piece of opposing color, if the movement of the man off the line of pin would expose a piece of greater value to capture. For example, a knight is said to be pinned by a bishop if the movement of the knight would expose the queen or a rook to capture.

In a problem, however, a man is pinned only when the king is on the line of pin, so that the pinned man never can move off the pinning line because the king would be left in check.

If a bishop is pinned along a diagonal, or a rook along a rank or file, it still can move on the line of pin and so is only *line-pinned*. A queen can never be absolutely pinned, but merely line-pinned, for whether pinned by a rook, bishop or the opposing queen, she always can move along the pinning line.

Pinning and its reverse, *unpinning,* play an important part in the mechanism of a large percentage of modern problems, particularly of *two-movers,* the name applied to problems in which white mates in two moves.

The second point to note in problem A is that, although the black king cannot move in the initial position, the black queen's rook can capture the white knight, vacating b8 so the king can move there. A square to which the black king can move is termed a *flight-square,* or more briefly, a *flight.*

To solve a problem, one method is first to examine all black's possible moves and to visualize what white's replies must be, with the supposition that a keymove has been made. In a two-mover, white's reply in every case must be a mate. This method will be used for problem A.

In this position one of the most natural defensive moves for black to make would be 1 —— RxS, which would give the black king b8 as a flight-square. Now the solver must figure out what change in the arrangement of the white men would be necessary to enable white to mate after

1 —— RxS. He will see that if the white rook were not on the seventh rank, white could then mate by 2 QxQ. This immediately gives a clue to the key. Perhaps it is a move by the rook, withdrawing to some square down the file; to d1, for instance (1 Rd1). This move leaves the white queen line-pinned by the black one, but the white queen can move along the line of pin and she threatens to mate by 2 Qd7. *if R does not take S x Q*

If R does not take S

Black can prevent the threatened mate by 1 —— Rc7, and this move illustrates another important problemistic feature. When the rook moves to c7, it cuts off the black bishop's guard on b6. Technically this is termed an *interference* of the rook on the bishop, and it permits white to mate by 2 Sb6, since the bishop no longer guards b6. Interferences are another mechanism frequently used in problem construction.

Although the black rook cannot effectively defend against the threatened mate by 1 —— Rc7, it can by playing onto the queen's file (1 —— Rd3), cutting off the white rook's guard on d7. But white can forestall this possible defense by not withdrawing the white rook so far. 1 Rd5 may be tried, and now white can mate on the next move despite the moves of either black rook.

Black can defend, however, in still another way. Playing the knight to f7 or the bishop to e7 will prevent the white queen from mating by 2 Qd7. Either of these moves *unpin* the white queen and allow her to move off the rank. So if 1 —— Sf7, white mates by 2 Qg4. If 1 —— Be7 the queen again is unpinned. Now she cannot safely play to g4, but she can capture the rook on c3. Yet this is not mate since black can interpose the bishop (2 —— Bc5).

Sx Q

If the white rook, however, had been withdrawn only to d6, the bishop would not be able to interpose at c5 after

If Bc7, then Qg8

1 — — Be7; 2 QxR. Besides the defenses that have been examined, there are no other moves black can make that prevent white's threatened mate, 2 Qd7. Accordingly 1 Rd6 must be the key to the problem, since there is no other first move that will lead to a mate in two moves despite any defense black can make. It is black's defense by 1 — — Be7 that determines the exact square to which the white rook must withdraw.

The key is theoretically good as it seems to limit white's potentialities, because it pins the white queen which is free initially. The key is said to *self-pin* the white queen, since the pinning is brought about by a move of a man of the same color.

In problem A the solver has seen examples of line-pins of a black piece and of a white piece, the latter effected by a self-pinning move (1 Rd6), two unpins of a white piece (1 — — Sf7 and 1 — — Be7), an interference (1 — — Rc7), and a defense by *square vacation* to give a flight, since after 1 — — RxS white can no longer mate by 2 Qd7 but must play 2 QxQ.

B

KENNETH S. HOWARD
The Falkirk Herald
March 30, 1927

White mates in two moves

In taking up problem B the two points to be noticed first are the complicated arrangement of pins and the fact that black has no possible move in the initial position.

It will be seen that the white bishop pins the black rook, which in turn pins the white queen, while the queen pins the black knight. The black rook and knight are absolutely pinned, and the white queen is line-pinned. Since black is in a stalemate position, the key must be a move that relieves the stalemate. This fact makes the problem easy to solve, as the key must release one of the black men.

A move of the white king or knight does not free black, and 1 BxR ck, PxB, clearly leads nowhere. Then it soon will be seen that if the black king is given a flight-square by a move of the rook, the king's bishop or the pawn, it will not be possible for white to mate on the second move. Consequently the key must be a move by the line-pinned queen, unpinning the black knight.

After 1 Qf7 white cannot mate on the second move, no matter how black plays. 1 Qf6 ck is met by 1 —— SxQ or 1 —— Ke3, and on 1 Qf5 the black king also escapes to e3. So by the mere process of elimination, the solver finds that 1 Qf3 must be the key. Even if the key may be found so readily, it is considered theoretically good because it unpins the black knight.

After 1 Qf3 no mate is threatened on the next move, and black would be safe if not forced to play. So this type of key is known as a *waiting move*. Now when the unpinned black knight makes any *random move*, one without any definite defensive purpose, such as 1 —— Sd2, 1 —— Sd6 or 1 —— Sg5, white can mate by 2 Rd5, since the removal of the knight from e4 permits the white queen to guard d5. Black can prevent this mate, however, by making a *correction move* (to use the technical term) with the knight.

Thus 1 —— Sc5 prevents the rook from reaching d5. This black move, on the debit side, *self-blocks* c5, so that the white rook no longer needs to guard that square, and white mates by 2 Rb4. Another way for black to defend against 2 Rd5 is by making the correction move, 1 —— Sc3, to which white retorts 2 PxS mate. Finally, black can guard against 2 Rd5 by 1 —— Sf6, but this move unpins the queen so that she can mate by 2 Qd3.

The last line of play is the one the composer primarily constructed the problem to illustrate, and it is called the *theme* of the problem. In this particular theme a line-pinned white piece (the queen) makes the keymove, unpinning a black man (the knight), which in turn unpins the key piece (the queen) and allows it to move *off* the line of pin to deliver mate.

In connection with problem B, new problemistic elements that have been brought to the solver's attention are examples of a waiting-move key, of random defensive and black correction moves, and of a self-block, and also an illustration of a typical problem theme.

C

KENNETH S. HOWARD
The Morning Post
October 8, 1932

White mates in two moves

In examining problem C it will be seen that the function of white's king's rook is probably to guard the sixth rank, while the white king and pawn aid in guarding the fourth rank, to prevent the black king from escaping. For a moment the solver may consider guarding the sixth rank by 1 Ra5 – a6, releasing the other rook to threaten mate by

2 Rh5, but black has adequate defenses in 1 —— Bd6 and 1 —— Pe6. So it seems likely that mate must be given by the queen's rook through a discovered check.

In the problemist's parlance an arrangement such as the knight on b5 and rook on a5 is termed a *battery,* of which the knight is the *firing piece.* Here the battery is "aimed" at the black king. In order for the knight to discover mate from the rook in this position, however, it first will be necessary to guard d4 with another piece, so that the black king cannot escape to that square when the knight on b5 is moved. It is apparent that the only practical way that this can be done is by using white's king's knight, and 1 Sc2 may be tried.

This move gives the black king two flight-squares, d5 and f5, and if he moves to either he will discover check to the white king from the bishop. These checks should not deter the solver from trying 1 Sc2 as the key, since perhaps the checks may be the point of the problem. After 1 —— Kd5 dis ck, the solver will find there is a mate by 2 Sc7, and after 1 —— Kf5 dis ck, a mate by 2 Sd6. In reply to 1 —— Kf5 dis ck, 2 Sc7 is not mate because black can interpose the pawn; so that white must play 2 Sd6 to mate by double check.

Such black checks to the white king countered by white moves that shut off the black checks and simultaneously check the black king, are termed *cross-checks.* White "crosses" the line of the black check and checks the black king at the same time. In a two-move problem the resulting check to the black king must be a mate.

In a cross-check both the black and white checks may be direct checks, or both may be checks by discovery, or one may be direct and the other by discovery. In this particular problem black gives discovered checks, while white gives double checks.

If black, instead of moving his king after 1 Sc2, moves his bishop, white simply captures the bishop with the knight. Likewise 1 —— Sa3 or 1 —— Sc3 is met by 2 SxS, while in response to 1 —— Sd2 any move of white's queen's knight discovers mate.

Yet before the problem can be considered solved there is one more black move to be examined, 1 —— Pe6. This shuts off the guard of white's king's rook on d6, so if the knight on b5 now discovers check the black king can escape to d6. This means that 1 Sc2 is not the key after all, but is only an excellent *try*, as first moves are termed which, while not solving a problem, lead to mates in several lines of play, or even to mates in every line but one, as 1 Sc2 does here.

The solver will see that white must put an additional guard on d6 as well as on d4, and so may try 1 Sf5. Now if 1 —— Pe6, any move of the knight on b5 mates. If 1—— KxS dis ck, the square d4 no longer needs to be guarded to enable white to mate by 2 Sd6. So 1 Sf5 is the key and the problem is solved.

When the black king can capture a white man he is said to have a *flight-capture*. So this key, 1 Sf5, gives the black king a flight-square at d5 and a flight-capture on f5.

The defensive moves of black that develop the thematic play of a problem are termed *thematic defenses*. In this problem the moves of the black king, discovering check, are the thematic defenses. The key is also *thematic*, because it makes it possible for the black king to discover the checks.

In problem A the key is thematic because it self-pins the white queen, while the moves of the black bishop and knight that unpin the queen are thematic defenses, as the self-pinning and subsequent unpinning of the queen constitute the theme the problem was composed to illustrate.

The key of problem B also is a thematic one, since it un-pins the black knight, which in turn makes a thematic defense when it unpins the queen; these consecutive un-pins being the theme of this problem.

Finally, problem C illustrates another feature; this time one that is regarded as objectionable from a constructional standpoint. A problem must have only one keymove, or it is unsound. Similarly, it is highly desirable that following each black move, white shall have only one possible reply leading to mate. Where white has a choice of two mating moves they are termed *duals*. Where there is a choice of more than two moves it is sometimes called a *triple* or a *multiple*, although commonly the word "dual" is used generically to cover any number of choices.

Duals vary in objectionableness, according to whether they affect the thematic play of the problem. When they do not and are merely of a trivial nature, they frequently are disregarded. On the other hand, if there is a dual in a thematic line of play, so that white need not make the thematic mate, the problem is spoiled.

After the keymove is made in problem C, white threat-ens to mate by playing the queen's knight to any one of six squares. Duals actually occur, however, only when black plays 1 —— Sd2 or 1 —— Pe6, and these moves do not affect the thematic play of the problem, which lies in the cross-checking lines of play. Any other move by black forces a single reply by white.

New terms brought to the solver's attention in connec-tion with problem C include battery, cross-check, try, flight-capture, thematic key, thematic defense and dual.

In problem D a cross-check is already *set*, as is termed a prearranged mating move by white following a black defense. The solver will note that 1 —— Bc8 ck is met by 2 Sd7 mate, since when the black bishop moves to c8 it

D

KENNETH S. HOWARD
Grand Rapids Herald
September 24, 1933

White mates in two moves

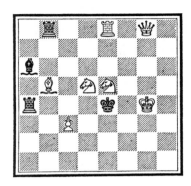

interferes with the black rook's attack on the white rook.

This set cross-check should suggest to the solver that cross-checking may be the theme of the problem, and if such is the case there probably is more than one of these checks. So the solver should look for another possible cross-check. In problem c the black king discovers check from a bishop. In this problem the black king could discover check from the rook on a4, if the king could move off the rank. In fact, the arrangement of the pieces, with the black rook on the same rank as the white king and only the black king intervening, would lead an experienced solver to suspect that the composer has planned for such a discovered check by black. In the initial position the black king cannot move, but perhaps the key may allow him to do so.

In seeking the key it must not be overlooked that white has to maintain a mating reply to the check by the black bishop. Black also has a strong defense in 1 —— RxR, which will leave white's king's knight unguarded. This consideration may be a guidepost to the key. Thus white may play 1 Qg5 to doubly guard e3, so that the knight's guard on e3 will no longer be necessary and mate will be threatened by 2 Sf6. This move of the queen will at the same time doubly guard the king's knight, making 1 — — RxR ineffective as a defense against the threatened mate.

With the queen on g5, if black plays 1 — — Bc8 ck, white still can mate by 2 Sd7, since the move of the king's knight now leaves the queen's knight guarded by the queen. An arrangement of men like that of the king's knight and the queen, after she has moved to g5, is called an *indirect battery,* because when the battery is fired by the moving of the knight, the queen guards a square adjacent to the one on which the black king stands, instead of attacking the king himself. The rook and knight form a *direct battery,* because the rook is on a line with the king and attacks the king (checks) when the knight moves.

The queen's move, 1 Qg5, unguards the queen's knight, thus giving the black king a flight-capture, 1 — — KxSd5, which enables him to discover the check that was suggested by the initial setting of the problem. When the king moves to d5 the knight-queen battery becomes a direct one and the knight-rook battery an indirect one. White counters the discovered check by 2 Sc4, shutting off the black rook and discovering mate from the queen. This move also opens the knight-rook indirect battery so that the rook now guards e4, preventing the return of the black king to that square. In addition, note that the move of the knight to c4 puts a guard on d6 to prevent the king's escape there.

Black has another defense not to be overlooked. 1 — — Rb6 defeats the threat of 2 Sf6, but white now retorts 2 Sc6, again firing both the direct and indirect batteries, and at the same time shutting off the black rook so it cannot interpose.

New terms that have been explained in connection with

problem D are set play, and direct and indirect batteries.

As a solver becomes more proficient he usually ceases to rely on any one particular solving procedure, and employs one of several methods according to the character of the problem on which he is working. Problem E is an excellent illustration of one that may be solved rather readily by either of two methods.

E

KENNETH S. HOWARD
V *British Chess Magazine*
August, 1932

White mates in two moves

One of the methods easy to apply to problem E is that of considering the probable use of the white men, taking up each one in turn and deciding whether it may be the one that makes the keymove.

It is evident the white king is placed on h8 so that the white queen will be line-pinned. The king cannot move without submitting to a check from the black rook. The white queen can move only along the line of pin, and any move except 1 Qg7 simply results in her capture. A moment's examination shows that 1 Qg7 is pointless.

1 Sf4 permits the black king to escape via f2. 1 Sg1 or 1 Sg5 threatens nothing. 1 Sf2 threatens 2 Sg4 mate, but 1 —— Bf5 is an adequate defense. So the solver may conclude that the purpose of the white knight is to guard f2

and f4, even though these squares are also guarded by the white queen.

The white pawn cannot move, and if the white king's bishop moves the black king can capture the white pawn. The white rook on a3 must not unpin the black queen, since it would permit 1 —— QxQ ck. If 1 RxQ ck, black replies 1 —— BxR, retaining the pin on the white queen. 1 Ra3–b3 threatens nothing.

By this rather rapid process of elimination, the solver sees that the keymove must be made either by the rook on b6 or by the bishop on b8. The rook seems out of play on b6, but a little experimenting will show that there is no way in which it can effectively attack as the position stands. 1 RxP pins black's rook and threatens 2 Bf4 mate, but black merely replies 1 —— RxR.

So it must be the bishop on b8 that makes the keymove and there are four possible bishop moves which have some promise. 1 Be5 unpins the white queen so that mate is threatened by 2 Qf2 or 2 Qf3, but 1 —— Bf5 prevents the queen from reaching either square. To meet 1 Bg3, or 1 Bh2, any move of the black rook, except 1 —— Rd4 or Re5, is sufficient, since a rook move vacates e5 and so gives the black king a flight square.

The only remaining move, with any likelihood of attacking possibilities, is 1 Ba7, setting up a rook battery, and if no oversights have been made in the elimination process, this move must be the key.

The second method is one that an experienced solver would be more apt to employ. On his first glance at the position, he would note that the white queen is line-pinned. This would lead him to suspect that the problem probably was composed to show unpins of the white queen by moves of the black men, allowing the queen to move off the line of pin and mate.

Next he would look to see how the queen may be un-pinned, and he would observe that unpinning may be ef-fected by a move of black's king's pawn and by two moves of the black rook. Making such black moves immediately, he would find mates set as follows: 1 —— Pe5; 2 Qf2: 1 —— Rd4; 2 Qf3: 1 —— Re5; 2 Qf4.

His final step would be to seek a keymove that would set up a threat to which these three black moves would be defenses. This would quickly lead him to try 1 Ba7, with the threat of 2 RxP, pinning the black rook so that it can-not defend the black king from the discovered check from the bishop. Each of the three black moves that have been examined prevent the threat from being a mate, but by unpinning the white queen they permit other mates.

Black moves that defeat a threat, with the ensuing mates, are known as *variations*. Variations that illustrate the theme of a problem are called *thematic variations*.

In problem E black has other defensive moves than those that unpin the white queen. One is 1 —— QxR (or 1 —— Qb3), which permits the black bishop to interpose on d4 on 2 RxP dis ck. To this defense white retorts 2 Rb6–b3 double ck. 1 —— Qd3 defeats the threat for the same reason and is met by 2 RxQ. These incidental lines of play, which are not related to the theme of the problem, are known as *secondary variations*.

When an experienced solver sees an arrangement of pawns similar to those in problem F, a white pawn on the second rank and black pawns on the fourth rank on both adjacent files, he will immediately advance the white pawn two squares, being confident that the problem illus-trates a theme based on en passant pawn captures.

After 1 Pd4, in problem F, white threatens mate by double check, 2 Rg3. Should black seek a flight square at g4 by playing 1 —— Pg3, the pawn then blocks the latter

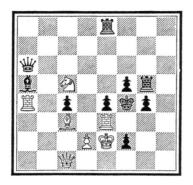

F

KENNETH S. HOWARD
Fifth Prize
Antony Guest Memorial Tourney
The Falkirk Herald
July 29, 1925

White mates in two moves

square, and there still is a mate by double check, 2 RxKP. The problem cannot be solved by 1 Pd3, because black will reply 1 —— BxB and e5 will be left unguarded.

The thematic defenses in this problem naturally will be the en passant captures of the white pawn, each of which results in check to the white king. If 1 —— BPxPep ck, white replies 2 RxQP. This is mate because black's king's pawn is now pinned by the rook on a4 and so cannot interpose.

If black plays 1 —— KPxPep ck, the pawn cannot be captured by the white rook because the latter is now pinned by the black rook on e8, but white can mate by 2 SxP, since black's queen's bishop's pawn is pinned and cannot recapture.

An arrangement of two black men on a line between the black king and a long-range white piece—queen, rook or bishop—is termed a *half-pin*. Neither black man is pinned in the initial position, but both may be considered as "half-pinned," because if either of the pair moves off the line the remaining one will be pinned.

Problem F competed in a tourney for two-movers in

which all the entries had to illustrate some half-pinning theme, and this position was composed to show en passant pawn captures made by each of a pair of half-pinned black pawns.

G

KENNETH S. HOWARD
Dagens Nyheder
September 1, 1935

White mates in two moves

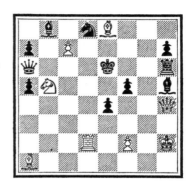

In looking at problem G the white pawn on the seventh rank should soon catch the solver's attention. This pawn can capture the bishop and promote to a queen, or other piece, but it cannot move to c8 nor can it capture the knight, because the black bishop pins it along the diagonal. Although 1 PxB=Q hardly seems a likely key for a modern problem, it should be examined by the solver, if for no other reason than to find black's defense. The promoted queen threatens to mate by 2 Qe5, and the only way that black can avoid this mate, or lay himself open to some other one, is by playing 1 —— BxB, which will give the king a flight-square at f7.

The noting of this possible black move is a good lead, since it seems so effective a defense that the solver naturally will look for a key that will provide a mate even if the white bishop is captured. If white could play PxS and claim a knight, it would check the black king and guard f7 at the same time, so that 1 —— BxB would not save black.

The pawn on c7, however, cannot capture the black knight and promote to a white one unless it is unpinned.

Usually in problems that have pinned white men, arranged so they can mate black when unpinned, the unpinning is brought about either by the withdrawal of the pinning piece or by the moving of another black man onto the line of pin.

In Problem G the bishop on b8 clearly cannot make an unpinning move, but black can unpin the white pawn by 1 —— Pf4, which would really be an interference on the bishop, even though in this instance the pinned white pawn is between the bishop and the interfering black pawn on the diagonal with the white king. The interference is actually with the bishop's power to pin the white pawn.

Should black play 1 —— Pf4, however, it would create a flight-square at f5, so that 2 PxS=S would not be a mate after all. This fact may lead the solver to observe that white will not be able to provide any mate following 1 —— Pf4.

Although it is not usual for white to make a keymove that unpins one of his own men, perhaps he does so in this problem. So far no use has been shown for white's king's bishop's pawn. If it were advanced two squares, 1 Pf4, it would prevent black from giving his king a flight by moving his own bishop's pawn to that square. It would also unpin the pawn on c7 to threaten mate by 2 PxS=S. So 1 Pf4 seems likely to be the key.

Since the solver already has seen en passant pawn captures used as thematic defenses in problem F, he naturally will examine the effect here of 1 —— PxPep. By thus removing white's king's bishop's pawn from the b8 – h2 diagonal, the pawn on c7 again becomes pinned and the

threatened mate is averted. Through the en passant capture, however, black has opened the king's file, and the arrival of the black pawn on f3 interferes with the bishop on
h5 so that white can mate by 2 Qe1. This line of play is so
striking that it should confirm the solver in his belief that
1 Pf4 is the key. Actually the problem was primarily composed to show this very line of play, so that it is called the
mainplay, or the thematic variation.

Black also can defend by moving the knight so that it
cannot be captured, but each move of the knight leads to
a new mate. 1 —— Sb7 interferes with the black queen's
guard on c8, so that white mates by 2 Pc8=Q. This promotion of the pawn on a different square, and to a different
piece than PxS=S, adds to the interest of the problem.

1 —— Sc6 interferes with the queen's guard on d6, and
the mate is 2 Rd6. 1 —— Sf7 self-blocks that square, so
that white can move the bishop and mate by 2 Bd7. Moves
of the black queen are met by one or another of the mates
already noted, and 1 —— BxP is answered by 2 SxB, a
mate that is set in the initial position.

The next position, problem H, is introduced to correct
an impression, prevalent among many solvers, that the
keymove of a problem must never be a capture. As previously explained, any legitimate move may be employed as
a key, but it is not desirable to select a move that is seemingly an aggressive one, or the kind of move a player
would naturally make in a game.

Ordinarily the capture of a black man would be such a
move and this has led many persons to look upon any
capture as a poor key. There was, in fact, a period of many
years during which even leading problem authorities
looked askance on capture keymoves, and problems entered in tourneys were penalized heavily whenever they
had such keys.

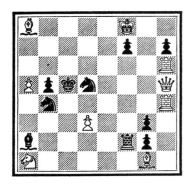

H

KENNETH S. HOWARD
The Pittsburgh Sun
September 19, 1925

White mates in two moves

Yet in certain cases a capture key may be the very opposite of an aggressive move; for example, where a white piece self-pins itself by capturing a black pawn and thus reduces its mobility. The capture of any black man other than a pawn, however, is regarded as too strong a move to be a satisfactory key.

In some instances the theme of the problem is based upon such a capture, which is the case in problem H. In this position mates are set for every black move except those of the bishop's pawn. The key is 1 QxP, but at first glance this does not look like a strong move for white, since it line-pins the white queen and at the same time unpins black's king's knight, thus seemingly increasing black's defensive possibilities. Furthermore, no mate is threatened by this keymove, but black is in *zugzwang* and any move he can make will weaken his position so that a mate results.

The thematic defenses are 1 —— Sf4 and 1 —— Sf6, which unpin the white queen and allow her to mate by playing 2 Qa7 and 2 Qe7 respectively. These are the thematic variations since the problem was composed to illustrate the Schór theme, in which a white piece unpins a black man and simultaneously self-pins itself, the unpinned black man then in turn unpinning the white piece, which moves off the line of pin and mates.

This is called the *Schór theme* because it was first brought to attention in a problem by the Hungarian composer, Lazzlo Schór. The theme illustrated in problem B is known as the *Howard theme* for a similar reason. There are scores of other themes, many much more complicated than these two, which are similarly distinguished by special names. Several of these themes are described in *Section Two*.

*

Ordinarily a solver does not tackle three-movers until he has had some experience in solving two-movers. Consequently, when he takes up three-movers, he usually has reached a stage where he can omit some of the more elemental steps he used when first solving two-movers. In fact, some of the more obvious points of a problem will perhaps be noted more or less subconsciously. As a rule the successful solving of three-movers depends more on the solver's ability to discern the idea that it is probable the composer is illustrating, rather than in the following of any mechanical procedure.

Thus the most proficient solver is apt to be the one who has developed his imagination so that from the general setting of a problem he can visualize its thematic possibilities.

In the three-mover, there being a sequence of five moves —three for white and two for black—it is possible to develop more strategical play based on a series of moves than can be shown in the two-mover. On the other hand, in the modern two-mover, moves often will be found that have manifold effects on several other men, whereas such complex results from a single move are far less common in three- and four-move problems.

The first three-mover to be examined, problem 1, is a lightweight position, white having only three men and black four. Problems with a total of seven or less men are called *miniatures,* this term being used more commonly in connection with three- and four-movers than with two-movers.

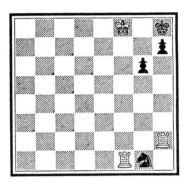

I

KENNETH S. HOWARD
American Chess Bulletin
September–October, 1925

White mates in three moves

The solution of this problem will be comparatively easy to work out, since white has so few first moves that are at all promising. At the start the solver will see that nothing can be gained by moving the white king to f7 and then attempting to mate with a rook on the eighth rank, because black can always release his king by Ph5.

Of course, the solver will not expect the key to be such an aggressive move as the capture of the knight, but it is well to see why the capture will not lead to mate. If 1 RxS black replies 1 —— Ph5. Then if 2 QRxP, Kh7 and there is no mate. Likewise after 1 Rf7, 1 —— Ph5 is an effective defense.

So the solver must find a line of play that Ph5 will not

defeat. Such a line is 1 Rf6, threatening 2 RxSP and 3 Rg8. After 2 RxSP the advance of the rook's pawn is ineffective. Black may play 1 —— Ph5, but white now continues 2 KRxP ck, PxR; 3 Rh6 mate, this variation being the "idea" of the problem. The solver will see that this is an idea that requires three moves to illustrate. Should black play 1 —— Sh3, white still continues 2 RxSP.

J

KENNETH S. HOWARD

V The Observer
August 24, 1924

White mates in three moves

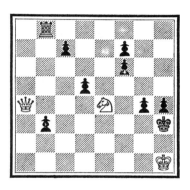

Problem J is another lightweight position, white having but three pieces. The solver will probably at once select the queen to make the keymove, since she is so obviously out of play in her initial location. Furthermore, the only possible king move, 1 Kg1, seems purposeless, and were the knight to move it would release a guard on a square in the black *king's field*, a name given to the square on which the king stands and those immediately adjacent to it.

Another reason the solver should not consider moving the knight is that composers do not like to use for a key a move which takes an en prise man out of danger, because such a move is just the kind that would be most natural to make in a game. In an occasional problem the composer has to resort to a key which withdraws a man from an attacked square, but the solver will not meet such a key very often.

In deciding to which square to move the queen, the solver will note that there are three which seem to offer good possibilities of bringing her into action promptly. 1 Qa1 threatens 2 Qf1 mate, but black has effective defenses in either 1 —— Pg3 or 1 —— PxS. 1 Qd4 may next be tried. This threatens 2 Qe3 ck, Pg3; 3 Sf2 mate. Here again 1 —— Pg3 prevents mate.

The third move that looks promising is 1 Qc6. This threatens 2 Qc3 ck, Pg3; 3 Sf2, resulting in a *pin-mate*, which is a mate where there is a pinned black man that could prevent the mate were it not for the pin. While this pin-mate is the most attractive mate in the problem, there are three other mates following black pawn moves which defeat white's threat, 2 Qc3 ck.

The most natural defense for black is 1 —— PxS, when white recaptures, 2 QxKP, and threatens 3 Qg2. Now if 2 —— Kg3; 3 Qe3, and if 2 —— Pg3; then 3 Qf5. Black can also defend against 2 Qc3 ck by 1 —— Pd4. In this case white continues 2 QxPf6, threatening 3 Qf1, and if 2 —— Pg3, again 3 Qf5 is mate.

The third defense is to play 1 —— Pg3 immediately. Now, however, this defense is not sufficient, as it was in the case of the tries 1 Qa1 and 1 Qd4, because the queen can reach d7 to check on the diagonal. Black must interpose a pawn on f5, and white captures it, mating.

While in the two previous three-movers there were no flight-squares for the black king, in problem к there are three, c6, d6 and e4. This is one of the first features of the problem that the solver should observe. To mate the king it is obvious that these squares must be guarded in addition to attacking d5 on which the king stands. Since three

K
KENNETH S. HOWARD
British Chess Magazine
August, 1924

White mates in three moves

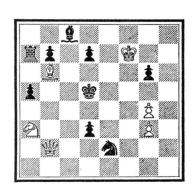

of the squares, c6, d5 and e4, are on the same diagonal, a check along the diagonal would cover all three. The only piece available for such a check is the queen, and so it is likely that the keymove is one which places the queen where she can reach the diagonal, possibly at h1.

As a first move the solver may try 1 Qa1. This move threatens 2 Qh1 ck, Kd6 or e5; 3 Sb4 mate. If 1 —— Ke4, the same second-move check is effective. But what if 1 —— Kc6? Now if 2 Qh1 ck, the black king captures the bishop and there is no mate. Before giving up the possibilities, however, a second move that is not a check may be tried. After 1 —— Kc6, 2 Qe5 brings the queen where she threatens mate by 3 Qc5. Now if 2 —— KxB; 3 Qd6 mate: if 2 —— Pd6; 3 Qb5 mate: if 2 —— Pd5; 3 Qc7 mate.

Should black nullify white's threat of 2 Qh1 ck, by playing 1 —— Sc1 or 1 —— Sg1 to prevent the queen from reaching h1, or by 1 —— Sf4 or 1 —— SxP to interpose or capture the queen if she checks from h1, the square d4 is left unguarded, so that white replies 2 Qd4 ck, Kc6; 3 Qc5 mate.

The problem is still not solved, however, because black has yet another defense in 1 —— Sc3, allowing the knight to interpose on e4 to a check by the queen from h1 and at the same time obstructing the a1–h8 diagonal to prevent 2 Qd4 ck. So apparently 1 Qa1 is not the key. Now the question for the solver is how to retain all the mating continuations that have been worked out and in addition to provide one to meet 1 —— Sc3.

The squares that the queen has to reach on one of her second moves are h1, e5 and d4. From what square, other than a1, can she play to these three squares? The answer is h8. After 1 Qh8, Sc3 still defends against the threat 2 Qh1 ck, but it does not prevent 2 Qd4 ck. So 1 Qh8 is the key.

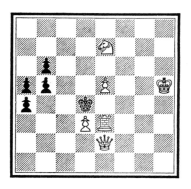

L

KENNETH S. HOWARD
The Pittsburgh Post
August 17, 1924

White mates in three moves

Problem L is a more difficult type to solve than the three preceding positions. Although white has such a relatively overwhelming force that at first glance it may look as if it should be easy to find a mate in three moves, there are no outstanding guideposts to the solution.

The first point to note is that the black king has two flight-squares and the solver should investigate to see what may happen when the king moves to these squares. If 1 —— Kc3, 2 Sc6 will confine the king to the third rank, so that the queen's pawn can discover mate on the next move, 3 Pd4. Then if 1 —— Kc5, the king can be confined to the fifth rank by 2 Re4, with a threat of mate by 3 Qc2. If black plays 2 —— Pb4, to give the king a flight-square, 3 Pd4 again mates, since now b4 is blocked by the black pawn.

Instead of moving the king, black may play 1 —— Pa3 or 1 —— Pb4, and no mating continuations are apparent. So the solver must arrange for mates following these pawn moves.

From the two mating continuations already found, it would seem unlikely that either the knight or queen should change its position, since both pieces are needed in their present locations. The rook might move along the rank, 1 Rf3, without disturbing its effectiveness when the black king moves, but no mate in three would follow if black responded with a pawn move.

The white king has appeared to be a mere innocent by-stander, but perhaps he is not. Were he not designed to take some part in the play, the composer might have placed him further from the scene of action. The solver may experiment by bringing him still nearer. 1 Kg4 is aggressive, in that it brings a white piece toward the black king, yet it seems but mildly belligerent.

Now, however, if black moves one of his pawns, white plays 2 Qc2, threatening 3 Re4 mate. If 2 —— KxR, the knight mates by 3 Sf5, as the white king guards f3 and f4. This variation shows why the white king must go to g4.

A feature that makes the solution of the problem difficult is that all white's second moves are *quiet,* a term applied to white continuations that are neither checks nor captures. Another feature that should be noted, is that during the course of the solution every white man moves, with the exception of the king's pawn.

*

The author believes that after this introduction to the elementary methods employed in solving chess problems, the reader will be ready to enjoy the selected compositions in *Section Two.*

Section Two

THE solver, who follows some definite method in solving chess problems, undoubtedly gets more enjoyment than does the solver who works in a haphazard way. The former, also, not only will solve more readily a larger proportion of the problems he tackles, but will be better qualified to appraise the merits of the positions.

Where no regular solving procedure is used, one solver may remark that he solved a certain problem at a glance, while the next solver will comment that he found the solution extremely difficult. Actually the solution may be neither especially simple nor especially subtle. One solver was lucky and happened to hit on the key quickly, and the other solver did not.

Occasionally a composer sets out to construct a problem for the express purpose of endeavoring to deceive the experienced solver. Today, however, the composition of such problems is rare, since most modern composers are chiefly interested in illustrating definite themes and difficulty of solution is a subordinate consideration.

It is undoubtedly true that American composers, as a whole, give more attention to attempting to provide unexpected keymoves than do many foreign problemists. In fact, where the keymove is not an essential part of the problem, there are numerous composers who will utilize for a key any conventional move that will yield a sound position.

Of course there are types of problems in which the

thematic content is primarily based on the key, such as those in which set play is changed by the keymove. In such problems the solver will find mates already arranged for all, or several, of the possible black moves, only to discover after the keymove is made that the set mates are replaced by other mating moves. The skillful composer will endeavor to disguise the nature of such problems as much as possible, since the solver's pleasure, to a large extent, will depend upon the degree of his surprise when he perceives the character of the changed play.

Even these problems may not prove difficult to the veteran solver, who has learned to recognize the general appearance of positions designed to feature changed play. Such a solver, however, will be interested to observe with what degree of skill the composer has succeeded in arranging the changes of play. In other words, the pleasure of the solver will come from appreciating the composer's mastery of technique.

Occasionally in the construction of a problem the composer will see an opportunity to work in a good try. Perhaps he will note that there are only two black moves which prevent a second solution. He may then reconstruct the problem so that only the more obscure of these black moves will still be a defense.

Such experiences, however, are not common occurrences. Actually in the illustration of the majority of the complicated themes in which the modern two-move composer is interested, the constructional difficulties are so great that the composer has little chance to alter the position merely to add a good try to the problem.

Experienced solvers use various methods in approaching problems and there is no one set procedure which can be recommended as an Open Sesame for solving all kinds of compositions. The purpose of this volume is merely to suggest some systematic approaches which a solver may adopt to aid him to solve more rapidly and with a keener appreciation of the excellencies of the problems.

As a solver grows more experienced, naturally he will note an increasing number of points on his first glance at a position, and in many cases he either will skip over various solving steps, or will telescope several into a single operation.

The methods that may be employed in solving two-movers differ somewhat from those ordinarily used for three-move or longer problems. So the solving of two-movers will be treated first. Since many of the procedures used for two-movers, however, are applicable to problems of any length, in taking up three- and four-move problems it only will be necessary to consider in detail the differences in method required by the increased length of the solution.

In endeavoring to solve a problem the solver may first examine its mechanical construction, or he may immediately seek to discover the theme the composer made the problem to illustrate. In actual practice the expert solver may utilize either method, or a combination of both, depending upon the appearance of the position. The first method may be termed Constructive Solving, and the second Thematic Solving.

An examination of the mechanism of a position often will disclose some constructional weakness, and in many instances such a defect will give a broad clue to the key. An example of a constructional defect is a white piece so obviously out of play in the initial position that the solver will see at once that in order to bring the piece into action it must make the keymove. This is solving from the observance of Constructive Weaknesses, and where such a weakness is present this method is often the quickest means of finding the key. Of course the method is only applicable where such weaknesses are apparent.

In constructional solving often one of the readiest ways to find the key is by the method of elimination. Beginning with the white king, the position of each white man is examined in turn and its probable use considered. Some white men may not be able to move without yielding too much freedom to black, while others may be free to do so without disrupting the position. In the latter case, it should be noted whether a white man can make an attacking or a seemingly purposeful move, or if its mobility is useless.

By this procedure it frequently will be seen in a few moments that the positions of the majority of the white men are unquestionably, fixed, so that the possibility of making the keymove narrows down to one or two men. The solver, however, must distinguish between moves which actually allow black too great freedom and those that merely seem improbable. In changed-mate problems especially, the composer may deliberately make it appear unlikely that a certain man is to be moved.

Checks and captures commonly can be disregarded as probable keymoves, although occasionally the key is a capture of a black pawn. In ordinary problems, pawn promotions, en passant pawn captures and castling will not occur as keys.

A second procedure, useful in many instances, is to begin by considering how the position will be affected by moves of the black men, especially of the black king if he has a flight square, and of black men located near him. If no mate is set for the black king's move onto a flight square, the key must provide a mate for such a move.

In a problem with half-pinned black men, the solver

should observe if mates are arranged to meet moves of the half-pinned men. Then he should seek a key that sets up a threat to which moves of the half-pinned men are defenses. This procedure lies on the border line between constructional and thematic solving.

In taking up illustrative two-movers in this section of the book, solving from Constructive Features will be considered first, using problems Nos. 1 to 14 as examples. Then a half dozen problems having Constructive Weaknesses, Nos. 15 to 20, will be examined.

Finally, Thematic Solving will be discussed in connection with Nos. 21 to 58. With a few exceptions, only general types of themes will be treated, and they will be handled somewhat according to their conspicuousness, rather than by any logical thematic relationship. Thus the first thematic group to be considered will be cross-check problems; which, as explained in the previous section, are problems in which black is allowed to check the white king in the course of the solution.

From a constructional standpoint two-movers may be divided into two general classes, according to whether the key sets up a direct threat of mate. Where it does, the problem is termed a *threat problem.* In the other class no mate is threatened after the keymove has been made, but a position results where any move black may make weakens the defense so that white can mate. Such a problem is called a *waiting move problem.*

In most cases the solver, after a little experience, can determine on his first glance at a problem whether it is of the threat or waiting move type. In a threat two-move problem no black moves have any bearing on the solution except those that are definite defenses against the threatened mate. Accordingly the composer may allow black any number of aimless moves in such positions and threat problems are usually characterized by the apparent freedom of movement of the black men.

For example, a black pawn may be located at a distance from other men with the probable purpose of interfering with the movement of a black piece so as to prevent the white king from being checked. If such a pawn is free to move without affecting the position, it indicates that the problem is of the threat type. Likewise a black queen, whose possible movements are not closely constricted, is usually indicative of a threat problem.

On the other hand, if black pawns are blocked, especially by opposing white ones, and if the liberty of movement of the black men in general appears to be restricted, the problem is probably of the waiting move type.

Perhaps the kind of two-mover that is most difficult to solve is a threat problem which has some set play changed by the key. If set mates are provided to meet some of black's apparently most likely defensive moves, the solver will not look for a possible changed play as he might in a waiting move problem. So he may be loath to give up such lines, especially if the mates set are attractive ones. Examples of such changed-mate play in threat problems will be found in No. 17, 25 and 50.

1

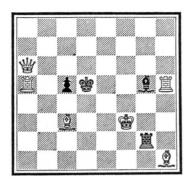

OTTO WURZBURG
American Chess Bulletin
September–October, 1939

White mates in two moves

WAITING MOVE PROBLEMS are again subdivided into *incomplete* and *complete block* positions. In the initial position of an incomplete block problem mates are set for some of black's possible moves, but not for all of them. So to solve an incomplete block a key must be found that provides mates for those moves of black for which mates are not already arranged.

Wurzburg's problem is a simple illustration. There is a mate set for every black move except 1 —— Rg1. So the key must provide a mate to follow this move, without disturbing other mating arrangements. 1 Ra2 meets the requirements, since after 1 —— Rg1, white now mates by 2 Rd2. This key unpins the black pawn, permitting black to play 1 —— Pc4, but white then mates by 2 Ra5. This is termed an *added mate,* and the move of the rook back to its original square is called a *switchback.*

2

ALEXANDER KISH
*Entry in Pawn-One-Two Tourney
American Chess Bulletin
May–June, 1936*

White mates in two moves

THIS PROBLEM illustrates two mates by discovery from moves of white's king's pawn. Hence the term, "pawn-one-two." It is also a good example of an incomplete block. In examining the position it is seen that if the black knight moves, white mates by 2 Bc2, and on 1 —— BxP white plays 2 SxB; but there are no mates set for other moves of the bishop. To provide such mates white plays 1 Bh5, so that 1 —— Bd2 will be met by 2 Pe3, and 1 —— Bf2, etc., by 2 Qd3.

This key, however, changes the mates after moves of the knight. 1 —— Sc2 is now followed by 2 Pe4, a second discovered mate by this pawn, while after any other knight move white mates by 2 Qb1. This replacement of a set mate by entirely different actual mates is considered a meritorious feature, and such a change is less expected in an incomplete than in a complete block position.

3

F. GAMAGE
V Third Prize
Open Section, Fourth Tourney
C. C. L. A., 1939

White mates in two moves

GAMAGE HAS USED the incomplete block setting for some of his finest compositions. No 3 illustrates the doubling of a highly strategic maneuver, but the theme is not apparent until the keymove is made. So the problem is not adapted to thematic solving. The arrangement does not immediately suggest an incomplete block position since there are only two set mates, and these follow unimportant black moves. The blocking, however, of the black pawn on a4 by a white pawn, which has no other use, indicates that the problem is probably a waiter.

It is fairly easy to solve this problem constructionally, because on examination it soon is evident that the white queen is the only piece which can make any effective first move, and her movement is restricted to the diagonal by the threatened check by the black knight. Note that black's thematic defenses are the pawn moves, 1 — — Pd2 and 1 — — Pe5.

4

F. GAMAGE
First Prize
American Chess Bulletin
Informal Tourney, 1940

White mates in two moves

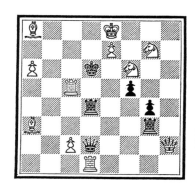

THE OPEN SETTING, comparative freedom of black's queen and queen's rook, and the few set mates in No. 4, tend to mislead the solver into looking for a key that threatens a mate. This masterpiece is one of the finest incomplete block two-movers ever composed and it is difficult to solve because of its deceptive construction. The experienced solver naturally will expect mates by discovery from the rook-bishop battery. In this connection he will note that such mates require either c7 or e5 to be guarded by a white piece other than the rook.

1 Kd8, guarding c7, is an excellent try, because the correct defense is not too apparent, especially since white has a mate following black's most conspicuous defense, 1 —— Qa5 ck. The solver will observe, however, that either 1 —— Qb4 or 1 —— Rb4 cuts off the support of the white rook on c5, so the keymove must provide for these defenses.

5

OTTO WURZBURG
The Atlanta Journal
September 29, 1939

White mates in two moves

IN A COMPLETE BLOCK problem there is a mate already provided for any move black can make. So if white can make a first move that will not disturb any of the mating arrangements, in other words "lose a move," the problem is solved. Few problems are constructed today, however, with such pure waiting move keys, because they can be solved too readily by the routine method of examining each possible white move in turn until one is found that does not upset any of the set mates.

In the modern complete block problem the key usually changes one or more set mates, and such problems are called *mutates,* a term coined by Brian Harley, chess editor of the London *Observer* and author of several books on chess. In No. 5 only one mate is changed, but both the key and the new mate are so striking that the problem is a memorable one.

6

WILLIAM A. BEERS
First Prize
American Chess Bulletin
Informal Tourney, 1939

White mates in two moves

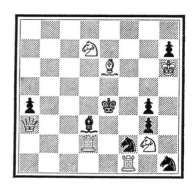

BEERS' PRIZE WINNER was composed to illustrate a definite theme, the self-pinning of black pieces by moves of the black king. The setting is that of a complete block, and the moves of the black king pin other black pieces so as to permit mate, viz., 1 —— Kd4; 2 Qb4, and 1 —— Kf3; 2 Bd5. White is unable to make any waiting move key, and the actual key changes one mate and adds another, the latter involving a third self-pin of a black piece, which makes the problem more interesting thematically.

The fact that the black pawns are blocked by white pieces should immediately suggest to the solver that the problem is a complete block. The pawn on h7 prevents the white king from making a waiting move, for if the king moves so does the pawn, and the king cannot capture the pawn because of 1 —— Kd4 or Kf3 dis ck.

7

OTTO WURZBURG
American Chess Bulletin
January, 1936

White mates in two moves

MANY MUTATES immediately disclose their character by blocked pawns, particularly if there are opposing white and black pawns, but the solver will have to look carefully at Wurzburg's gem to realize that the position is a complete block. The pawns on a5 and c5 obviously are employed to restrict the black king, and at first glance the locations of the white king and queen do not appear to be fixed. This is the ideal form of construction for a mutate. In the actual solution two mates are changed and one is added. Note that one white knight takes over the mating duties of its fellow, a constructional device often used in problems of this kind.

Two-movers having twelve or less men are called *Merediths,* after the Philadelphian composer, William Meredith (1835–1903), who favored lightweight compositions. This problem, and also No. 1 and No. 2, are Merediths.

8

VINCENT L. EATON
*American Chess Bulletin
September–October, 1943*

White mates in two moves

IN THE INITIAL POSITION OF NO. 8 a mate is set for any move black may make, but it will soon be seen that white has no waiting move, nor is there any way merely to change some of the mates. A clue to the solution lies in the pinned black bishop, which seems useless except to prevent the white king from making a waiting move. The key sets up a mating threat, changing the entire nature of the play.

This type of problem is called a *block-threat,* because it has the setting of a complete block but really is a threat problem. Much attention was given to such problems some thirty years ago. Their composition, however, has been limited, both because of the great constructive difficulties involved in securing satisfactory settings and of the trend toward the illustration of themes based on strategic rather than on constructional features.

9

KENNETH S. HOWARD
American Chess Bulletin
November–December, 1939

White mates in two moves

IN A THREAT PROBLEM the keymove sets up a definite threat of mate, either by the man that makes the keymove or by another one. No. 9 shows a threat in most simple dress. The solver will see that the only likely first move is 1 Bg5, threatening 2 Bh6 mate. There is nothing of interest in this and the threat is employed merely to force the thematic black defenses, 1 —— Pe6 and 1 —— Pe5, which produce the strategic play of the problem. A large percentage of threat problems have keys of this kind, whose only function is to bring black's thematic defenses into action.

The two pawn moves permit the white queen safely to unpin the black one, and to deliver two long-range mates. This maneuver constitutes the *Gamage theme,* named after a famous problem composed by F. Gamage. No. 9 was constructed to show the theme in the lightest possible setting.

10

BURNEY M.
MARSHALL
American Chess Bulletin
January–February, 1939

White mates in two moves

UNLIKE NO. 9, the mating threat in Marshall's problem is from another piece than the one that makes the keymove. Where a second man threatens the mate, the solution often is less apparent and more subtle than it is where the same man that makes the keymove threatens to mate.

Marshall composed this problem to show three unpins by black of the white queen. The key is thematic because it self-pins the white queen, which the black defenses then unpin. In solving, the finding of the key is only a first step; the solver should also work out all the thematic or major lines of play in a problem. In this particular composition there is no play outside of the threat and the three thematic unpinning variations. The mates initially following moves of the black bishop vanish in the actual solution, a feature that may mislead the solver.

11

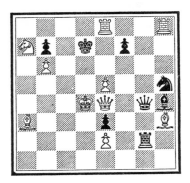

GEOFFREY
MOTT-SMITH
V *American Chess Bulletin*
March–April, 1942

White mates in two moves

THE OPPOSING WHITE and black pawns in No. 11 may lead the solver to assume that the position is a block, but he soon will note that the pawn on b6 is to guard c7 and the one on e2 is to prevent a check to the white king. The opposing pawns merely happen to be on adjacent squares. Here again the brilliant keymove is made by a different piece than the one that threatens mate, which may add some difficulty to the solution. The problem illustrates play by two line-pinned queens. As explained in *Section One*, a queen cannot be absolutely pinned since she always can move along the line of pin and so is only line-pinned. One of the thematic lines of No. 11 is in the threat itself and a second one is produced by 1 —— Qe6. Black's secondary defenses, 1 —— Sf4, 1 —— Pf5 and 1 —— Sf6, should not be overlooked.

12

F. GAMAGE
*First Honorable Mention
American Chess Bulletin
Informal Tourney, 1941*

White mates in two moves

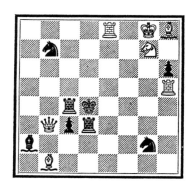

A PLEASING FEATURE of Gamage's beautiful composition is that the piece which gives mate in the threat also delivers the mates in the two thematic variations. Thus the threat mate is linked to the thematic play, and this gives a satisfying unity to the problem. This problem is a third example where mate is threatened by a different man than the key-piece.

Black's two thematic defenses and the succeeding white mating moves show an identical type of play on different squares. Such repetition of a defense, of a mate, or of an entire variation, is termed an *echo.* The mates in the two thematic variations are also *self-interference mates,* since the white mating piece interferes with a white guard which is no longer required, because the black defenses self-block squares next to the black king that white previously had to keep guarded.

13

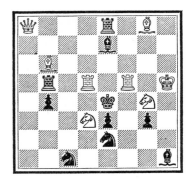

F. GAMAGE
First Prize
American Chess Bulletin
Informal Tourney, 1943

White mates in two moves

BATTERIES WERE DESCRIBED in *Section One* in connection with problems c and d. A battery is an arrangement of two men of the same color on a line, where a *front* man temporarily obstructs the action of a *rear* long-range piece —queen, rook or bishop. When the front man moves off the line the battery fires. A direct battery is aimed at the king of opposite color; an indirect battery at a square adjacent to the king. Direct batteries have been seen in problems 2, 3, 4 and 12. In problem 1 a black man is also on the battery line and this arrangement is termed a *masked battery*.

When the experienced solver sees a battery, he studies how it may be brought into effective action. No. 13 illustrates a typical use of a direct battery, the rook moving to four different squares to discover mate from the queen.

14

E. NEUHAUS, JR.
American Chess Bulletin
September–October, 1940

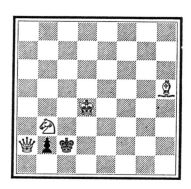

White mates in two moves

NO. 14 IS AN EXAMPLE of a type of position where the construction gives an immediate clue to the solution, but not because of any constructive defect. The first glance at the problem shows that black is in a stalemate position, and so the key must be a move that relieves the stalemate. Although this problem does not exhibit any strategic novelty, it is notable for the extreme lightness of the setting. The waiting move key leads to four lines of play, one of which ends in a switchback mate.

The black pawn promotion to queen or to knight, with two different mates, is the most interesting feature of the problem, whereas these same defenses appear in the more complex No. 20 merely as incidental variations. While the solution presents little difficulty, a position like this delights the solver because of its daintiness.

15

WALTER JACOBS
American Chess Bulletin
November–December, 1941

White mates in two moves

IN MANY PROBLEMS there is some constructive weakness that gives a clue to the solution, and the next few positions are given as examples that can readily be solved by observing a weakness in construction.

Ordinarily the first thing an experienced solver notes in examining a position is whether the black king can move, or has a flight, technically speaking. Whenever there is a flight-square it is highly desirable to have a mate already set if the king moves onto it. Otherwise it is termed an *unprovided flight,* which is regarded as a constructive defect. When a solver finds an unprovided flight, he should at once look for a keymove that will produce a mate when the black king occupies the flight-square. In problem 15 there is no mate set for 1 —— Ke5, and so the solver should seek a key that will provide a mate after this defense.

16

GILBERT DOBBS
Second Honorable Mention
(ex aequo)
British Chess Magazine
Informal Tourney, July–December,
1939

White mates in two moves

IN NO. 16 THE UNGUARDED KNIGHT on d6, in the black king's
field, provides a possible flight-capture, a term explained
in connection with problem c in *Section One*. Should no
mate be set for a flight-capture, it is regarded as even
more of a constructional weakness than is a mere unprovided flight.

The meritorious features of a problem, however, may
so far over-balance a constructional weakness of this kind
that it becomes negligible, except as a guide to the solution. In No. 15, for example, the key had the offsetting
merit of permitting the white king to be checked. In the
present attractive composition the solver will at once note
black's checks, 1 — — Qe3, etc., and 1 — — Qg7, met by
2 Sd4 and 2 Se7 respectively. The key adds a third thematic variation. Nevertheless the veteran solver will immediately realize that he must find a key which will provide a mate after 1 — — KxSd6.

17

KENNETH S. HOWARD
American Chess Bulletin
January–February, 1939

White mates in two moves

IN PROBLEM 17 AGAIN there is an unprovided flight-capture, 1 —— KxP. When the solver first examines this position, however, his attention will probably be equally attracted by this point and by the black checks, 1 —— Qb8 ck and 1 —— QxP ck, met respectively by 2 Se8 and 2 Sd5. These are cross-checking variations, as explained in *Section One.* Cross-checks frequently are made the theme of a two-move problem, and in such a case there usually are two or more of them. In Dr. Dobbs' No. 16 there were three cross-checks, the knight defending the white king and simultaneously discovering mate from the bishop.

The unprovided flight-capture in No. 17 unquestionably is a weakness in construction, but the position has off-setting features so that this defect may not immediately give away the solution. The solver should not overlook white's rook-bishop battery.

18

F. GAMAGE

First Prize (ex aequo)
Cross-Check Section,
Fourth Tourney
C. C. L. A., 1939

White mates in two moves

A BLACK CHECK for which no mate is provided is regarded as a still greater constructional weakness than is an unprovided flight-capture, yet *unprovided checks* are occasionally found in a problem with sufficient compensating features so that the position may even win a prize. An example is Gamage's No. 18.

Mates are set for 1 —— Qe4 ck and 1 —— Qg1 ck, and for the discovered checks from the black bishop, with the exception of 1 —— Bd5 ck. The solver will see that besides discovering check from the rook, this move cuts off the white queen's guard on c6. He next will note that the white bishop on a3 is manifestly out of play. So he may try 1 Pb5, which guards c6, puts the bishop into play, threatens a mate by 2 Sb7, and provides a mate for 1 —— Bd5 ck. The constructional weakness of the unprovided check is more than offset by the four distinct cross-check variations.

GILBERT DOBBS
First Prize
Open Section, Fourth Tourney
C. C. L. A., 1939

White mates in two moves

IN NO. 19 WHITE'S QUEEN'S BISHOP is obviously out of play. The solver may first consider 1 Ba5 or Bb4; but when he sees that neither of these moves is effective, he will be led to push the queen's pawn, so that a double check can be given from the rook-bishop battery. This move has the further feature of self-pinning the white queen. The expert solver, who is solving thematically, seeing the two queens on a diagonal with the white king, will try 1 Pd5 just because it self-pins the white queen, expecting her to be unpinned in turn by one of black's moves.

In this fine composition the beauty of the mating moves overshadows any constructional weakness of the key. The problem should not be regarded as solved until the play is worked out in all six variations, in addition to the threat.

20

ALEXANDER KISH
*First Prize
American Chess Bulletin
Pawn-One-Two Tourney, 1936*

White mates in two moves

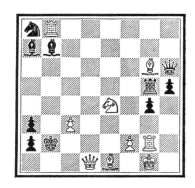

WHEN PROBLEM 20 IS EXAMINED it will be seen that white's king's bishop cannot be of any value in the attack until the diagonal is cleared by the removal of the knight, and even then the bishop can serve only as an additional guard for b1 and c2. Hence if the knight is moved, the knight itself must set up the mating threat. This reasoning gives a definite clue to the key, so that this position is an excellent example of a problem that is most readily solved by noting a constructional weakness.

As a problem this prize winner is notable for the thematic play after the key has been made. Each of black's two thematic defenses, in addition to directly defending the threat, opens one line of guard and closes another. In other words, each of these moves has a three-way black effect.

21

F. GAMAGE
*First Prize
Cross-Check Section,
Third Tourney
C. C. L. A., 1938*

White mates in two moves

IN SOLVING THEMATICALLY the solver endeavors to determine from his initial examination of the position the type of thematic play the composer is illustrating. Then he seeks the keymove necessary to make the scheme work. Frequently this is a readier method of solving than to search for some weakness in construction.

One of the general themes easiest to recognize from the arrangement of the men is the cross-check, of which several examples have already been examined. In No. 21 note the relative positions of the white king and black's king's bishop. If the knight on d4 were not pinned it could discover check. So the expert solver will experiment by unpinning the knight by 1 Sc4 or 1 Se4. Since the former is met by two obvious defenses, he will decide on 1 Se4, which threatens 2 Rf4. Then he will look for mates following each of the discovered checks from the black knight.

22

WALTER JACOBS
American Chess Bulletin
November–December, 1938

White mates in two moves

IN NO. 22 THE BLACK BISHOP on the same diagonal as the white king again suggests a cross-check theme, even though there is also a white piece on the line. So the solver may consider moving the white queen off the line. 1 Qg3 seems a plausible move because it threatens mate by the double check, 2 Re4. Now any move of black's king's knight will discover check, but at the same time it will leave the black rook pinned. So if 1 —— SxR ck or 1 —— Sc6 ck, white can mate by 2 Rf2, interposing on the line of check and discovering mate from the queen, since the black rook is pinned.

Black can prevent 2 Rf2, however, by 1 —— Sf3 ck, obstructing the f-file. In this case white can mate by 2 Rd4, as the black rook may now be safely unpinned because the knight interferes with RxQ. This complex variation is known as the *Goethart theme.*

23

ALEXANDER KISH
First Prize
Cross-Check Section,
First Tourney
C. C. L. A., 1936

White mates in two moves

KISH'S PRIZE WINNER also shows the white king on a line with a long-range black piece, with a white and a black piece intervening. This time the pieces are on a file rather than a diagonal. Any arrangement of this kind, however, should suggest to the solver the possibility of cross-check play. Of course the composer may intend black to defend by a move of the knight that will pin the queen, and 1 Qf4 may be tried, keeping the queen on the file. This move threatens both 2 Qc4 and 2 Qd4, but black can defend either by 1 — — PxR or by 1 — — Sd1.

Four other queen moves threaten mate. Against 1 Qa7 or 1 Qg7 black can utilize the same defenses; while after 1 Qf6, 1 — — Sg4 also becomes effective. None of these moves is a defense, however, to 1 Qc7. Note that the three discovered checks, 1 — — Sd1, 1 — — Se4 and 1 — — Sg4 each require different mating moves.

24

OTTO WURZBURG
*Third Honorable Mention
American Chess Bulletin
Informal Tourney, 1942*

White mates in two moves

IN THE LAST THREE PROBLEMS, all illustrating cross-check play, black cannot check until the keymove is made. Since black's checks and white's replies constitute the theme, the keymoves are thematic because they make possible the theme play. The key made the checks possible in No. 21 by unpinning the black knight, and in Nos. 22 and 23 by moving a white piece off the potential line of check. The key of No. 24 is more subtle, since the nature of the theme is not so clearly indicated by the setting. The two white batteries, however, may give a broad hint to the expert solver.

When black plays 1 —— Bf5, the bishop makes an interference on the rook on g5, preventing it from capturing the white bishop. Then when 1 —— Rg1–g2, the rook interferes with the bishop, so the latter no longer attacks the white rook.

25

BURNEY M.
MARSHALL
The Atlanta Journal
October 27, 1939

White mates in two moves

IN THIS BRILLIANT COMPOSITION by Marshall the cross-checking line may prove to be quite misleading. Because of the open setting the solver will decide that the problem is of the threat type; then he will see the set cross-check, 1 —— Pd4 ck; 2 Rf3. The theme of the problem is based on the black check, but the solver may be surprised when he discovers the denouement. This form of problem, that is built around one outstandingly striking line of play, with an unexpected keymove, undoubtedly is one of the most difficult kinds of two-mover to solve. After this problem has been solved it should be compared thematically with No. 17.

The thematic line in No. 25 is especially satisfying aesthetically because the actual thematic mate, with its *shut-off* of two black pieces, is strategically superior to the set mate that it replaces.

26

G E O R G E   B.   S P E N C E R
First Prize
Chess Review
Decalet Tourney, 1943

White mates in two moves

PROBABLY THE FIRST THING the solver will notice in No. 26 is black's check, 1 —— Qd1 ck, which can be countered by 2 Rf1, since the movement of the black queen has opened white lines of guard on h3 and h4. Next the solver may see that 1 —— QxR is met by 2 QxQ. Then perhaps he will observe the two unprovided checks, 1 —— KxP dis ck and 1 —— Kh4 dis ck. In the "Decalet" tourney each problem had to have exactly ten men, and this restriction naturally influenced the constructive features of many of the entries.

When the solver endeavors to work out mates to meet the checks discovered by the black king he will find that a second battery is required for the purpose, and this will change surprisingly the mate after 1 —— Qd1 ck. A further interesting feature of this composition is the effective pinning of the black queen in three lines of play.

27

KENNETH S. HOWARD
American Chess Bulletin
September–October, 1938

White mates in two moves

IN NO. 27 THE SOLVER will observe the two checks by the
black queen, 1 —— QxPc4 ck and 1 —— QxPf4 ck, in
each case self-pinning herself so that white can mate by
2 Be6 and 2 Bf5 respectively.

When a veteran solver sees the two white bishops on
the seventh rank between the black queen and the white
king he is likely to suspect an unpinning theme, and so will
look for a thematic key. Such a key would be a move by
the queen's bishop leaving the king's bishop pinned. Then
the black queen's self-pinning checks would unpin the
king's bishop and permit it to interpose and simultaneously discover mate. With this clue it only remains to
find a square for the queen's bishop that will set up a
mating threat. When a pinned man is unpinned by the
withdrawal of the pinning piece, it is termed a *withdrawal
unpin*.

28

CHARLES W.
SHEPPARD
First Commended
American Chess Bulletin
Informal Tourney, 1944

White mates in two moves

AFTER SOLVING NO. 27, the solver naturally will notice the somewhat similar battery in No. 28. In No. 27 the black queen unpinned a bishop, which could then mate by discovering check because the black queen had self-pinned herself and could not interpose. But if the queen in No. 28 unpins the bishop by withdrawal, there is no way by which she can self-pin herself, and the unpinning of the bishop will be ineffective unless some means can be found to prevent the queen from interposing on the line of the subsequent check. Should black play either 1 —— QxP or 1 —— QxS, however, the unpinned bishop could then pin the queen and mate would result.

After the solver has proceeded thus far, his next objective will be to find a first move that will set up a mating threat to which 1 —— QxP and 1 —— QxS are defenses. There are some incidental variations.

29

OSCAR E. VINJE
The Observer
January 30, 1938

White mates in two moves

THE TWO PINNED WHITE PIECES in No. 29 suggest an unpinning theme, with withdrawal unpins by each of the black pinning pieces. To solve the problem a threat needs to be found that can be prevented by a move of the bishop on e6 or of the rook on g2, which will draw one or the other off its line of pin. The solver will note that the one square to which both can move is g4. What white threat will a man on g4 defeat? What about 1 Bh5, threatening 2 Rf3? If 1 —— Bg4, unpinning the queen and interfering with the black rook, then 2 Qg5. If 1 —— Rg4, unpinning the knight and interfering with the black bishop, then 2 Sh3.

This interference on each other by the moves of the black bishop and rook to g4 is known as a *mutual Grimshaw interference,* after a problem published in 1850 by the English composer, Walter Grimshaw.

30

BURNEY M.
MARSHALL

*Second Honorable Mention
American Chess Bulletin
Informal Tourney, 1939*

White mates in two moves

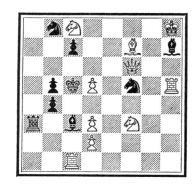

IN A PROBLEM FEATURING unpinning, instead of having a
pinned white man unpinned by the withdrawal of the
pinning piece, it may be unpinned by the move of a second
black man onto the line of pin, as has already been shown
in problems A, B, E, H, 10, 11, 13, 19, 20. This is called an
interference unpin, and it occurs in No. 30 when black
plays 1 —— Sd4 or 1 —— Sg7. In any problem having a
pinned white man, the solver should suspect a possible unpinning theme.

Since the theme of No. 30 is apparent, to determine the
key it is necessary to find a move to which 1 —— Sd4 and
1 —— Sg7 are defenses. Such a move is not obvious, until
the solver realizes that the bishop on h7 may have some
purpose other than to guard the black knight. If the knight
moves the bishop will guard e4. Why should black wish
to guard e4?

31

ERIC M. HASSBERG
*First Commended
American Chess Bulletin
Informal Tourney, 1943*

White mates in two moves

THE UNPINNING PROBLEMS examined so far have shown un-pins of white men by black's moves. In the initial position of No. 31 it is a black piece which is the pinned man. In problems featuring the unpinning of a white man, a thematic key is one that pins the man originally, as in No. 10 and No. 27. Theoretically white weakens his position by thus restricting the power of one of his pieces. Conversely, in a problem where a black man is initially pinned, a key that unpins the black man would be a thematic one.

In No. 31 the black queen might be unpinned by a withdrawal move of the white rook, but an interference unpin by the move of another white piece onto the line of pin is a more likely procedure. Further pinning and unpinning is involved in the complex main-play, which illustrates the *Hassberg theme.*

32

KENNETH S. HOWARD
*V American Chess Bulletin
January–February, 1939*

White mates in two moves

THE MOST NOTICEABLE FEATURE of No. 32 is that both queens are line-pinned, which has already been seen in problem 11. In the present instance the solver will naturally suspect another unpinning theme. He will observe that a move to d4 by either black knight or the pawn will unpin both queens simultaneously. The reason for playing a black man to that square probably will be to unpin the black queen so that she can defend a threatened mate. What threat can white make which a free black queen can prevent?

When the key has been found by following this line of reasoning, the solver should work out the variations produced by the moves of each black knight and of the pawn to d4, and ascertain why each of these moves forces the unpinned white queen to mate on a different square.

33

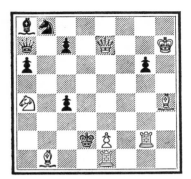

WALTER JACOBS
British Chess Magazine
January, 1933

White mates in two moves

THE ARRANGEMENT OF THE MEN on the seventh rank in Jacobs' classic composition suggests that black may defend a threatened mate by moving the pawn on c7, pinning the white queen. It also is apparent that the movement of this pawn will interfere with the guarding action either of the black bishop or queen along the diagonals. If a pin of the white queen will defeat the threat, the threat must be a mate delivered by the white queen herself. Accordingly the solver should look for a keymove that will enable the queen to mate. The position is set so economically that the locations of most of the white pieces are fixed. Consequently the key should not be hard to discover, though it is an excellent one.

The moves of the pawn on c7 produce the thematic defenses and they are met by corresponding moves of the white pawn.

34

ERIC M. HASSBERG
V American Chess Bulletin
July–August, 1942

White mates in two moves

PROBLEM 34 SHOWS an arrangement along the c3 – h8 diagonal similar to that along the seventh rank in No. 33. This suggests either a cross-check theme, following a key that takes the white queen off the diagonal, or a theme in which black's defenses are rook moves that leave the white queen pinned. Since white has no battery, nor other obvious means, to counter black checks, the theme cannot be a cross-checking one, but probably is based on pins of the white queen. So the solver should look for a keymove leading to a threat to which pins of the queen will be defenses.

If the black rook makes a random move, a term explained in connection with problem B, white threatens mate by 2 Qd4. This is known as a *contingent threat*. Black, however, can forestall this mate by 1 —— Rd5 or 1 —— Re4. These are correction moves and force other white replies.

35

CHARLES W.
SHEPPARD

*First Honorable Mention
American Chess Bulletin
Informal Tourney, 1944*

White mates in two moves

AS EXPLAINED in *Section One,* two black men on a line between the black king and a long-range white piece are *half-pinned,* because if either moves off the line the man that remains is pinned. The resulting mates, if truly thematic, could be prevented by the unmoved black man were it not for the pin. These are called pin-mates, as previously mentioned. Often the easiest way to solve problems with half-pinned men is by investigating the half-pin play.

Half-pinning often can be combined with other elements in elaborately constructed problems, of which No. 35 is a beautiful example. Each of the half-pinned black knights can defeat the threat by making a random move, and then again defeat white's contingent threat by a correction move. Both correction moves have four-way effects (described in detail on pages 92 and 93) and result in half-pin mates.

36

F. GAMAGE
First Prize
American Chess Bulletin
Informal Tourney, 1942

White mates in two moves

HALF-PINS ARE *heterogeneous* when the half-pinned men are of different kinds, as in problems 4, 18, 19 and 22; *homogeneous* when they are of the same kind, as in problems F, 35, 36, 37 and 43.

To solve No. 36 figure out the defensive reasons for moving the half-pinned black knights. Moving the king's knight permits the black bishop to guard f6. Why should black guard f6? Might not white's king's rook threaten mate there if it were supported? The only practical way to support the rook is by 1 Ke7. Any move of black's queen's knight, however, leaves the rook pinned so it cannot mate. Nevertheless 1 Ke7 looks like the key. After random moves of either black knight 2 Be6 is the contingent threat. To defeat this threat the white bishop can be shut off by correction moves by either black knight, 1 — — Sb3 or 1 — — Sc4, each being followed by a thematic half-pin mate.

37

WALTER JACOBS
First Honorable Mention
American Chess Bulletin
Informal Tourney, 1942

White mates in two moves

ALTHOUGH ENTIRELY DIFFERENT thematically from No. 36, Jacobs' problem can be solved in a similar way. Moves of the half-pinned knights open diagonals for the queen or bishop as in No. 36. Moving the knight on e5 permits the black queen to guard the pawn on f4. So the key may be a white queen move attacking this pawn. Moving the knight on e7 lets the black bishop guard g5. While the white knight can check on g5, in the initial position this move interferes with the white's queen's guard on f5. Yet these considerations should be sufficient to determine the key.

Actually the key sets up two threats, ordinarily considered a defect, but here the essence of the theme. Random moves of either knight defeat one threat but permit the other to operate. Each knight, however, can make a correction move that thwarts both threats, leading to new mates.

38

ALEXANDER KISH
American Chess Bulletin
January, 1936

White mates in two moves

IN HALF-PIN PLAY black self-pins either one of a half-pinned pair by withdrawing its fellow from the potential line of pin. Such a move is termed self-pinning by withdrawal. Another type of black self-pin is produced by the capture of a white man on a line between the black king and a long-range white piece.

In No. 38 the pawn on e4 can be captured by three different black pieces, self-pinning the capturing piece, and pin-mates follow each capture. When the solver observes this, he will decide that it must be the kernel of the problem, and so he will seek a key that will set up a threat against which these captures will be the thematic defenses. The theme of the problem permits a multiple illustration, and it is named the *Schiffmann Defense* after the brilliant Roumanian composer who developed it.

39

WALTER JACOBS
*Second Commended
American Chess Bulletin
Informal Tourney, 1942*

White mates in two moves

IN NO. 39 THE EXPERIENCED SOLVER will note at once the possible cross-check, and so probably without hesitation he will try unpinning the black knight by 1 Se5 – d3. He will see that this move at the same time sets up the mating threat of 2 Qd5. If the unpinned black knight moves, discovering check, it clears the diagonal for the bishop on b1 to guard the knight on d3, permitting the other white knight to defend the check by playing to e2 and simultaneously discovering mate from the rook.

This mate is effective after any move of the black knight except the self-pin, 1 —— SxP. Now 2 Se2 ck will again unpin the black knight and enable it to defeat the mate by 2 —— Sg4. This is another illustration of the Schiffmann Defense. So in response to 1 —— SxP white plays 2 Sb2, a brilliant denouement. The secondary variations are not of thematic interest.

40

KENNETH S. HOWARD
The Observer
July 13, 1941

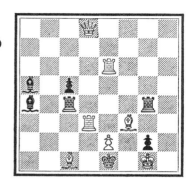

White mates in two moves

IN EXAMINING NO. 40 the solver will soon notice the two possible checks by the queen. He should endeavor to figure how these checks may become mates. In the initial position each check is defended by both black rooks.

When the solution is found it will be seen that the thematic defenses are related to those in problems 38 and 39. In the thematic defenses of those problems black self-pins a piece, and should white attempt to carry out the threat, the pinned man would become unpinned and prevent the mate. In the thematic variations in No. 40 black self-line-pins a piece, and it thwarts the threat because it can still move along the line of pin. In two secondary defenses a rook interferes with each bishop in turn, but these variations are not related to the theme and are present merely to make the position sound.

41

VINCENT L. EATON
*V American Chess Bulletin
January–February, 1940*

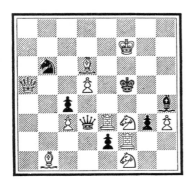

White mates in two moves

ALTHOUGH THERE SEEM to be two white batteries in No. 41, further examination shows that neither can fire effectively. So if they cannot be employed to check the black king, their only other possible purpose would be to permit a black man to self-pin itself by a capture. Since 1 —— SxP obviously has no defensive value, it must be the black queen which self-pins herself, and to be able to do so she must be unpinned by the keymove.

This process of reasoning leads logically to the thematic 1 Re4. This key not only permits the queen to self-pin herself by the capture of pawn, rook or knight, but also provides a fourth pin of the queen by 1 —— KxR. In problem 38 three black pieces self-pinned themselves by capture of the same white pawn; while here a single piece makes three self-pinning captures.

42

GEOFFREY
MOTT-SMITH
*Second Honorable Mention
American Chess Bulletin
Informal Tourney, 1942*

White mates in two moves

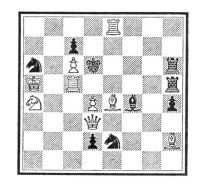

IN PROBLEM 42 the line-pinned piece is the feature that the solver probably will first observe. Then he will note the set mate, 1 —— RxR ck; 2 PxR. Naturally he will expect some strategical play from the pinned white rook, but he will see that in the initial position it only can be unpinned by 1 —— Be5, and no mate by the rook follows. This may suggest moving the rook, and the one square to which it can safely be played is e5. Now mate is threatened by 2 Rd8.

1 Re5 unpins the black bishop, which then can move to g5 and defeat the threat. This move, however, unpins the white rook and permits mate by 2 Re5 – e6. This variation is the thematic one, and the complete line of play, 1 Re5, Bg5; 2 Re5 – e6, constitutes the Howard theme. This theme is also illustrated in problem B in *Section One*.

43

WALTER JACOBS
First Prize
American Chess Bulletin
Informal Tourney, 1944

White mates in two moves

THE BEAUTIFUL NO. 43 is so economically set that the experienced solver may find its solution relatively easier than many a less perfectly constructed problem. To such a solver it will be apparent that the thematic mates will be given by the line-pinned white rook, and also that the squares to which the rook moves to deliver mate will be determined by moves of one or the other of the half-pinned black rooks. Actually the white rook mates on five different squares.

Obviously the white king cannot make the keymove. White's queen's rook must maintain the half-pin. 1 Sc5 is met by 1 —— QxS; 1 S elsewhere by 1 —— QxR ck. A queen move off the diagonal is similarly met. If 1 BxS or 1 Bd3, black simply captures the bishop, and any move of white's king's rook will then leave e4 unguarded. After this process of elimination the really excellent key should be apparent.

44

ALAIN WHITE
American Chess Bulletin
January–February, 1942

White mates in two moves

IN THIS COMPLEX PROBLEM there is a line-pinned white queen and a line-pinned black rook on adjacent ranks. With both these pieces line-pinned it is probable that the thematic play of the problem involves moves by each of them.

In the initial position white's queen's knight can check at e2, but this move interferes with the white rook's guard on e5. What if white first otherwise guards e5? This can be done by a move of the white queen along the line of pin, 1 Qc3. The line-pinned black rook, however, can then cut off the white queen's guard on e5 by 1 —— Rd4; but this move interferes with the black queen's guard on e3, and so white can mate by a second move of the line-pinned queen, 2 Qe3. Thus all the moves in the main-play of this remarkable composition are made by line-pinned pieces; keymove, defense, mate.

45

EDGAR HOLLADAY
Second Honorable Mention
American Chess Bulletin
Informal Tourney, 1944

White mates in two moves

NO. 45 IS A PROBLEM which perhaps may be solved most readily by first considering the possible defensive uses of the black pieces. The black knight on b3, for instance, has apparently no use except to play to c5 or d4, for which mates are set, viz., 1 —— Sc5; 2 Rd6, and 1 —— Sd4; 2 Pe4. The only purpose of these knight moves would be to continue with 2 —— Se6. This at first suggests that the key may be a move of white's queen's bishop, but the resulting threat of 2 Qe6 is defeated by 1 —— Pc5. This may lead the solver, however, to look for some other way for the queen to threaten mate, which also will provide a defensive use for the black rook on g2.

The problem theme is battery play combined with self-interference mates, which were explained in connection with problem 12. The knight defenses turn out to be merely secondary lines.

46

KENNETH S. HOWARD
American Chess Bulletin
November–December, 1942

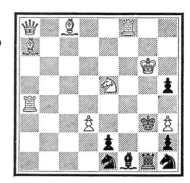

White mates in two moves

IF THE SOLVER analyzes the functions of the white men in No. 46 the knight will seem useless. True it guards f3 and g4, but these squares are otherwise guarded doubly and triply respectively. Furthermore the knight cannot be moved so that it can mate on the second move. It may occur to the solver that the knight may be made the firing piece of a battery. Yet even if a battery is set up no mate will be threatened.

A waiting move position will result, and following self-blocks of the black king the knight can discover mate, interfering in turn with whichever white piece is no longer required as a guard. This is an example of self-interference mates treated as the theme of a problem. The idea of this problem was anticipated in a problem by Shinkman, published in 1897, but the author considers No. 46 constructionally superior.

47

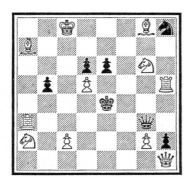

ALAIN WHITE
American Chess Bulletin
November–December, 1941

White mates in two moves

PROBLEM 47 IS a remarkable composition, which may prove puzzling even to the expert solver, until he notices that the white pawns on c2 and g2 have a symmetrical relationship to the black king. In his first examination of the position the solver's attention naturally will be focused on the pawn-queen battery, and he will note that its action is controlled by the black queen in such a way that the pawn may deliver four mates, three by discovery and one direct by capture. The set play is 1 —— QxS; 2 Pg3: 1 —— Qg5; 2 Pg4: 1 —— Qh3; 2 PxQ: 1 —— Qf3; 2 PxQ. No keymove and threat, however, will be found that will bring about this set play.

The theme of the problem lies in having the actual play feature the same kind of mates as those in the set play, so that each series of mates is in effect an echo of the other.

48

F. GAMAGE

First Prize
The Falkirk Herald
John Keeble Memorial Tourney,
1940

White mates in two moves

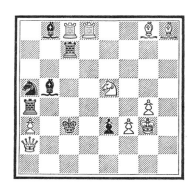

WHEN A SOLVER sees a direct battery in a two-move problem, usually he can assume that the battery will be utilized for mating moves. That is the reason the keys of problems 17 and 47 are especially deceptive, since they substitute new batteries for the ones in the initial positions.

In a problem constructed like No. 48, however, it may be taken for granted that the knight-bishop battery functions on the mating move, since there is no way in which this battery can be changed. So one good way to find the solution is to start by working out the battery mates. If 1 — — RxPg4 ck; 2 SxR: 1 — — RxPa3; 2 Sd3: 1 — — Bc4; 2 Sf7: 1 — — Bd7; 2 Sc4. Now the solver's task is to find a threatened mate to which these black moves will be defenses. When the key is found the solver may be surprised to discover that one of the set mates is changed.

49

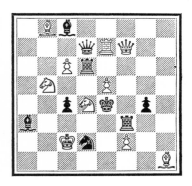

F. GAMAGE
*Third Commended
American Chess Bulletin
Informal Tourney, 1942*

White mates in two moves

THE FIRST FEATURE that may attract the solver in No. 49 is the pinned black rook on f3, and a moment's inspection will show that it is not obvious how it may be unpinned. Then the solver may notice the positions of the other white bishop and black rook and note that the latter would become pinned if the black king could capture the pawn on e5. Observe that this pawn and the white rook form a type of pawn-rook battery that only can be fired by a capturing move of the pawn to take it off the file. Perhaps the easiest way to find the key will be by experimenting with this battery.

The theme of this problem is the unpinning of one and the pinning of the other of a pair of similar black men, brought about by a move of the black king.

50

EDGAR THEIMER
*American Chess Bulletin
September–October, 1939*

White mates in two moves

IN MANY PROBLEMS the interplay of the black men is the feature that first attracts the solver's attention, especially where there apparently are cumulative effects. For example, in inspecting No. 50 the solver's eye will be focused at once on the square f6, since it is a square next to the black king to which black may play any one of three pieces, queen, knight or bishop.

Naturally the solver will try 1 —— Qf6 ck, because of the check, and he will see the set mate, 2 Bf5. Then he will observe 1 —— Sf6; 2 Bf7, providing a second mate from the bishop-rook battery. There is no mate set for 1 —— Bf6, however, and so the solver should look for a key that threatens a mate to which 1 —— Bf6 is a defense. He will find that the really excellent key accentuates the point of black's various moves to f6, and adds a thematic variation.

51

JULIUS BUCHWALD
First Prize
American Chess Bulletin
Informal Tourney, 1946

White mates in two moves

ONE METHOD, often applicable for solving two-movers, is to see what mates, if any, are allowed by the movements of the black men. In No. 51 if the black knight makes a random move, white mates by 2 Qd2. Black can defend against this mate by 1 — — Se4, but this permits 2 Qd3. 1 — — SxP prevents both these mates but allows 2 SxS. No mates, however, are set for any moves of the black bishops or the black pawn.

If the solver then turns to the white pieces he will note that all of them, except the queen, appear to be required for guard duty from the squares on which they stand. The seeming freedom of movement of the black bishops leads the solver to expect a threat problem, and from his analysis of the functions of the men he will decide that the queen must make the keymove. When the key is discerned it will be found that the position illustrates changed-mate play, the new mates being more interesting than those set in the initial position.

52

BURNEY M.
MARSHALL
First Honorable Mention
American Chess Bulletin
Informal Tourney, 1939

White mates in two moves

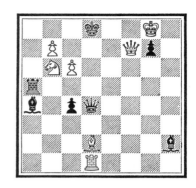

MARSHALL'S NO. 52 may not readily be recognized as a study in black interferences, or at least not until the purpose of the bishop-rook battery is understood. The key may be more than ordinarily difficult to find by thematic solving, although to the experienced solver the relative positions of the black queen, rook and king's bishop may suggest interferences. Probably the easiest way of finding the key is by studying the possible use of the battery.

Contrary to the usual form of direct battery where the firing piece discovers a check from the rear piece, in this battery the firing piece gives direct checks and the rear piece simultaneously immobilizes the black queen so that she cannot defend the checks. Ordinarily in problems showing similar interferences the queen is pinned in the initial position. The neat secondary variation, 1 —— Re5, should not be overlooked.

53

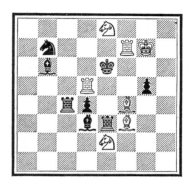

EDGAR HOLLADAY
Third Commended
American Chess Bulletin
Informal Tourney, 1943

White mates in two moves

IN EXAMINING NO. 53 the relative positions of the black rooks and bishops are suggestive. Thus the movement of a black rook or bishop to e4 cuts off the line of play of white's king's bishop along the f3 – d5 diagonal. At the same time these moves form a mutual Grimshaw interference. 1 —— Be4 permits 2 Re5. 1 —— Re4 would make 2 Bg4 a mate if white's queen's rook did not have to be guarded.

What if the rook were first withdrawn to b5, for instance? This would threaten 2 Bd5, to which the black moves obstructing e4 would be defenses. Similarly a move of a black piece to c5, cutting off the guard of the white rook on d5 would prevent the threatened mate. 1 —— Rc5, however, permits 2 SxP, and 1 —— Bc5 permits 2 Sc7. These black moves produce a second mutual Grimshaw interference. Finally, 1 —— Sc5 is an additional interference variation for good measure.

54

GEOFFREY
MOTT-SMITH
American Chess Bulletin
November–December, 1942

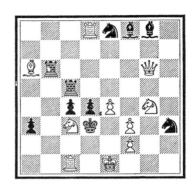

White mates in two moves

AGAIN IN NO. 54 the relative positions of the black rooks and bishops suggest a black interference theme, and one good way to solve this problem is to see if mates are already set for the interferences. 1 —— Bd5; 2 Se5, and 1 —— Bd6; 2 Pe5, follow interferences of the bishops on the rooks, but no mates are set for 1 —— Rd5 and 1 —— Rd6. So a key must be found that will threaten a mate to which these interferences will be defenses, and at the same time provide mates for the rook interferences on the bishops.

The four interferences between the black rooks and bishops constitute a double mutual Grimshaw. A similar problem by the author was honored in an Australian tourney in 1926. In composing No. 54 Mott-Smith was not aware of the earlier problem, and the author prefers to preserve Mott-Smith's version since it is the better of the two.

55

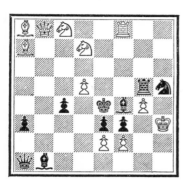

EDGAR HOLLADAY
Third Honorable Mention
American Chess Bulletin
Informal Tourney, 1943

White mates in two moves

IN NO. 55 IT WILL be noticed that either the black rook or bishop may play to e5, and in each case one black piece will interfere with the other, allowing mate by 2 Sd6 and 2 Pd6 respectively. The black queen also may play to e5, preventing both of these mates, but permitting 2 QxB. When the solver has made these observations the next step is to find a move that will provoke black to move a piece to e5. Further examination will show that a mate must be provided to meet 1 —— BPxP, and this should give a broad clue to the key.

Where a white piece is sacrificed so that black has a choice of capturing it with a rook or bishop, and the capture by either of these pieces will interfere with the action of the other one, the maneuver is known as a *Nowotny interference*. Here the captures produce self-blocks, followed by self-interference mates.

56

WALTER JACOBS
First Prize
American Chess Bulletin
Informal Tourney, 1941

White mates in two moves

THE LOCATION of the black knight on d5 in Jacobs' prize-
winner suggests a *line opening and closing* theme, especially since there are no pins nor batteries, nor possibility
of cross-checks. Furthermore two such mates are already
set: 1 —— Sc3; 2 RxR, and 1 —— Se3; 2 Rf4.

In the actual solution these defenses turn out to be the
thematic variations, and black's moves have a fourfold line
opening and closing effect, although this is not fully apparent until the key has been made. The opening of a potential line of flight for the black king counts as a line
opening for black, even though white never actually permits a flight. Such a black move is a defense, if it forces a
white man to retain its guard on that particular square.
Thus the vacating of d5 by the knight may prevent a
threatened mate by a move of the white queen elsewhere.

CHARLES W.
SHEPPARD
*First Honorable Mention
American Chess Bulletin
Informal Tourney, 1943*

White mates in two moves

THE POSITIONS of the long-range white pieces suggest that
No. 57 may also feature line openings and closings, in
which the black knights undoubtedly are the protagonists.
Any move of either black knight opens lines for the black
queen and also opens a3 – d6 for white so that the unmoved black knight is pinned. Four-way line opening and
closing effects follow 1 — — Sc6, 1 — — Sb7 and 1 — —
Sd7. These defenses should be carefully noted as they
are the ones in which the interest of the problem centers.

In the solution any random move of either black knight
defeats the threat but allows 2 Se4 to become effective as
a contingent threat. The moves of the black knights mentioned in the first paragraph are corrections that also defeat the contingent threat. To find the key the solver has
to discover a threat that will be met by any move of either
black knight.

58

KENNETH S. HOWARD
American Chess Bulletin
July–August, 1935

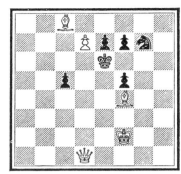

White mates in two moves

IF SOLVING by constructive weaknesses, the solver would note the unprovided flight in No. 58 and look for a key-move that would provide a mate to meet 1 —— Kf6.

It is more likely, however, that the white pawn on the seventh rank will catch his eye first. The relation of this pawn to the black king, and the bishop on c8, indicates that one mate, at least, will be by pawn promotion. Pawn promotion mates have already been shown in problem G on page 19 where there are promotions to queen and to knight on different squares. Probably there are also two such mates in No. 58, since a modern two-mover hardly would be constructed to show a single promotion mate. The solver accordingly should seek a key to bring about defenses to which these promotion mates will be replies. He will find the theme is promotion to a knight on two adjacent squares.

WHILE the procedure for solving three-move problems is similar in many ways to that for two-movers, there is a difference in the relative importance of various points, occasioned chiefly by the additional move allowed both white and black in the three-mover.

In examining two-movers the solver's first step usually is to note whether the composition appears to be a waiting move or a threat problem. Three-movers, however, commonly are threat problems, a waiting move three-mover being rather a rarity. Accordingly the solver usually takes it for granted that a three-mover has a threat, unless the setting definitely suggests a block position. Consequently, since only an occasional three-mover is a block, few of them can be solved by any mechanical routine without resorting to an unnecessarily detailed analysis.

When taking up a three-move problem the experienced solver judges, from the general appearance of the position, whether it has been composed to illustrate some form of strategy in the moves leading to the mates, or for the beauty of the mating positions themselves. Sometimes both of these objectives are combined in one problem, but such instances are exceptional.

Where the aim of the composer is centered on showing some interesting type of strategy in white's attack, in black's defense, or in both combined, the problem is termed a *strategic* one.

In the other general class of three-move problem the beauty of mating positions is the *raison. d'être*. In compositions of this kind there usually will be two, three or more model mate positions. Such problems are termed *model mate problems,* especially in distinction from *strategic problems.*

A *model mate* is a mate in which the square on which the black king stands and each adjoining square, constituting the black king's field, is guarded or blocked only once, and every white piece on the board takes part in the mate, with the possible exception of the white king, whose employment is optional.

Some authorities hold that any white pawn likewise, that is used in the problem, must guard a square in the black king's field to make a mate a model. Others do not subscribe to so difficult a canon of construction, but make the employment of white pawns in the mate optional, like that of the white king.

Nowadays a problem seldom will be composed for the specific illustration of mating positions unless they are models. An occasional exception to this custom occurs where a problem is constructed to show the echoing of an interesting mate that is not a model. Echoed mates are ones that have a striking similarity in the arrangement of the mating forces, but in which there is a difference in the square on which the black king stands, or in the men by which the mate is delivered, or a change in the squares on which such men stand, or a change in the guards of the king's field. An echoed mate of this kind in a two-mover is illustrated in problem 12 by the moves, 1 Re7, Rc5; 2 Sf5, and 1 —— Re3; 2 Se6.

Some three-movers disclose their nature at a glance, as, for example, most problems that feature en passant pawn captures, such as No. 64. Other three-movers do not reveal their type so obviously, although usually it is not difficult to decide from the appearance of a position whether the problem was composed for strategic play or for attractive mates.

An open setting, with relatively few black pieces, frequently indicates a problem in which the interest will center in the mating positions. This is especially apt to be the case if the black king has one or more flight-squares. On the other hand, a problem with numerous black men, particularly black pieces, suggests a theme in which black maneuvers probably take a prominent part, and in which the chief point of interest will be in the play rather than in the mating positions. Problems with only a few men often are more difficult to solve than are more complicated appearing compositions, because the lighter positions have less guideposts.

There are numerous kinds of settings that immediately suggest the strategic nature of a problem. Many of these types will be recognized at once by the veteran solver. Even to a solver with less experience, but who is somewhat familiar with two-move motifs, certain positions of the men will clearly indicate what character of play may be expected.

For example, a position where there is a black pawn that can promote on black's first move, especially if the black king is near the pawn, is clearly suggestive of a black pawn promotion theme. The pawn actually may be placed there for another purpose, such as to block a square or to interfere with the movement of some long-range piece. Or, even if it does promote, the promotion may be only an incidental defense. Yet the mere fact that it can be promoted should lead the solver to investigate whether the theme of the problem may not be based on such promotion play.

Another type of position that frequently, in a similar way, reveals the nature of the theme, is one where there is a white pawn that can promote on white's first or second move. A pawn promotion is rarely used as a keymove, because ordinarily it would be too aggressive to be a good key, since it would increase the strength of the white forces. So if there is a white pawn on its seventh rank it is more likely designed to promote on white's second move.

When the solver observes such a pawn, he should consider the possibility of its promotion to some piece other than a queen, or to different pieces to meet various black defenses. The solver should also note if the rest of the setting points toward a theme related to white pawn promotions. If it does not, the pawn may have been placed on its seventh rank for some merely incidental purpose.

When an examination of a problem shows long-range black pieces placed so that their lines of movement intersect, the likelihood of a theme based on black interferences is indicated. The solver already has seen illustrations of various forms of black interferences in the two-move field, such as the examples of mutual Grimshaws in problems 29, 51, 53 and 54, and of the Nowotny interference in problem 55.

In some three-movers the principal motif is cross-checking and the probability of such play is often apparent from the initial setting, as it is in the case of two-movers when the white king is on a line with a long-range black piece, with one man, or perhaps two, intervening. Problems 65 to 70, inclusive, have cross-checks; the cross-checking play being blended with en passant pawn captures in the first three.

Where the theme of a problem is not sufficiently pronounced to be immediately recognizable, the solver may follow an empirical method, as outlined in the following paragraphs.

If there are any flight-squares for the black king, the solver first should investigate what may occur when the king moves onto such squares. As a second step, he should examine the position of the white king. If the white king is liable to a check on black's second move, it usually indicates that white's second move threat must be a checking move to forestall the possibility of any black check.

When, however, there is no likelihood of the white king being checked, white's second move threat need not necessarily be a check but may be a quiet move. Of course there are exceptions to this, since the theme of the problem may involve checks to the white king which may be allowed by white's second move, or even by the keymove.

After the position of the white king has been examined, those of each of the other white pieces should be scrutinized in turn, and then the reason for each white pawn also should be determined. By noting the apparent use of each white man and finding which ones seemingly must retain their positions, the keymove often can be found by elimination.

The purpose of each black man should next be considered. Some black men may be employed merely to make the problem sound, but the location of others may afford an important clue to the theme of the problem, especially if the theme is one that is developed from the interplay of black men. If there are black pieces whose moves can interfere with each other's lines of guard, the possible results of such interferences should be studied carefully.

Finally, constructive weaknesses should not be overlooked. These may not be as revealing as in two-movers, because the extra length of the solution may afford offsets to many constructive shortcomings. In a two-mover, for instance, a piece may be so obviously out of play that the solver sees at once that it must be brought into play on the first move. That is, it must make the keymove. In a three-mover a piece equally out of play may not need to be brought into action until a later move. In fact, perhaps the black king may move toward it, and possibly it may have some effect on the play without moving at all.

Model mate problems often require a somewhat different solving procedure than does the usual strategic composition, although the suggestions made in the preceding paragraphs will be helpful in solving any type of three-mover.

The fascination of a model mate probably is partially due to the fact that it takes the solver a moment or more to realize that the black king actually is mated, when no more force is utilized than just exactly enough to produce a mate.

In a problem composed to illustrate model mates, there ordinarily should be at least three different lines of play ending in models, to justify the composition. It is not difficult to compose a problem containing two model mating positions, but it generally takes a considerable degree of constructive skill to arrange three or more of such mates.

An exception may be made in the case of model mates that are echoes of each other, since the echoing of model mates of any degree of complexity is often quite a feat, and two such echoing mates may provide a sufficient artistic content for a problem.

In solving a problem that apparently is a model mate composition, the solver should be on the lookout for possible model mating positions. Where there is a flight-square in the initial setting, the solver should immediately look to see what may happen if the black king moves onto that square, and should particularly investigate the possibility of such a move leading to a model mate.

When the solver has found a line of play that ends in a model mate, he should look for variations that may terminate in other model mates, since, as already explained, there usually are three or more such mates in a modern model mate three-mover.

OTTO WURZBURG
First Prize
Sam Loyd Memorial Tourney
Chess Review, 1942

White mates in three moves

THE SETTING OF NO. 59 suggests that it probably is an example of a strategic problem. The black king is confined to a corner square by the white bishop and one of the rooks. The other rook is free for attacking purposes, but there is a black queen to defend the king. So the theme of the problem undoubtedly is based on getting the black queen to play to some square where her guard will become ineffective. Note that the rook can threaten an attack both on the h-file and on the eighth rank, so the queen must endeavor to parry a two-way threat.

Observe also that the capture of the queen, without a check, produces stalemate, a device frequently employed by composers in positions of this kind. Compositions in which the black king is located on a corner square are sometimes called *king-in-the-corner* problems.

60

OTTO WURZBURG
First Prize
American Chess Bulletin
Informal Tourney, 1947

White mates in three moves

TO FIND THE KEY to No. 60, probably the simplest procedure is to investigate the function of each white piece in turn. The white king is apparently placed on a5 to block black's rook's pawn. The location of the white queen enables her to control both b7 and b8. Moving the bishop off the long diagonal would permit 1 — — Pb6 ck, and moving the bishop along that diagonal does not lead to anything.

By this process of elimination it would seem that the white rook must make the keymove. If 1 RxS, black simply plays 1 — — Pc4. While 1 Rb6 increases the attack on the knight's pawn, it does not threaten mate in two more moves. Other rook moves along the rank to d6, f6 or h6 are met by 1 — — Se6. This leaves 1 Rc6, which certainly appears most unpromising until white's startling second-move threat is discovered. Two of the ensuing mates are pin-models. This problem is a constructive masterpiece.

61

HENRY WALD
BETTMANN
*American Chess Bulletin
July–August, 1935*

White mates in three moves

THE WHITE PAWNS on the seventh rank in No. 61 indicate that pawn promotions undoubtedly are the chief feature of this miniature. In a problem of this kind the key may be relatively easy to find, since the composer unquestionably had difficulty in securing a sound position, as is shown by the placing of the queen behind the knight's pawn, so as to restrict her mobility to some extent. The key is a strong "playing" move, less objectionable here than in most problems, because the point of this composition lies in the echoing of the pawn promotion play.

As pointed out in connection with problem 12, echoing lines occur when the same, or a closely similar, type of play is repeated in two or more variations. In this problem there are such echoing lines when black continues 1 — — Kc8 or 1 — — Ke8. This is one of the last problems Dr. Bettmann published.

62

OTTO WURZBURG
First Commended
American Chess Bulletin
Informal Tourney, 1941

White mates in three moves

THE WHITE PAWN IN NO. 62 also indicates promotion play. In examining this miniature the solver will soon decide that the pawn promotion must take place on the first move. The key illustrates what is known as a *minor promotion,* which is a promotion to a piece other than a queen. When a rook or bishop is chosen in preference to a queen it is because there is some line of play where the queen would produce stalemate. In the present instance, if 1 Pa8=Q, Kf1; 2 QxP, black is stalemated. So this line of play is the reason for a minor promotion. A particularly attractive feature of this problem is that both continuations end in model mates.

In practical solving, pawn promotions to other pieces rather than to a queen are to be expected, since there is little of interest in such a normal move as a promotion to a queen.

63

GILBERT DOBBS
American Chess Bulletin
March–April, 1942

White mates in three moves

IN NO. 63 A MATING line is already set: 1 —— Ke6; 2 Bc6, any; 3 Qf6. The solution may prove the more difficult if the solver hesitates to abandon this promising variation.

If 1 —— Kc5, however, no mate follows such a move as 2 Qc4 ck, because the black king escapes via b6 to the seventh rank. At this point the solver may realize that there might be a mate if the black king were driven toward the white one. So he may try reversing the situation by 1 Qf6. This gives the black king a flight-square at e4 in lieu of e6, and if 1 —— Ke4 white mates by 2 Bc4 and 3 Qf4, similarly to the set line which is given up. The replacing of a set line of play by another one, often found in two-movers, is a rarity in three-movers. The problem was composed to show echoing mating positions, which should be worked out.

64

KENNETH S. HOWARD
American Chess Bulletin
May–June, 1938

White mates in three moves

AS POINTED OUT in connection with problem F, a pawn arrangement like that in No. 64, with a white pawn on the second rank on d2 and black pawns on the fourth rank on each adjoining file, suggests as en passant pawn capture theme. The solver will see that there is a similar relationship between the black pawn on d7 and the white pawns on c5 and e5. The part that the white pawn on f2 and the black one on f7 play in the scheme may not be so immediately apparent.

En passant pawn captures frequently produce striking effects in the opening and closing of lines, both for white and black. Problem 64, however, was composed merely to illustrate cumulative en passant captures and, outside of white line openings, no other strategic elements are blended with the captures. It is a study in such captures both by black and white.

65

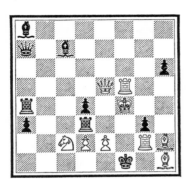

VINCENT L. EATON
American Chess Bulletin
May–June, 1938

White mates in three moves

ALTHOUGH IN PROBLEM 65 only one en passant capture can be made if white advances his king's pawn two squares, the general setting indicates the probability of this move as the key. The very fact that the en passant pawn capture will subject the white king to a discovered check from black's queen's rook makes it all the more likely that 1 Pe4 is the composer's idea.

Note the line opening and closing effects brought about by 1 —— PxPep dis ck. This move opens the line a4–f4 for black, but it closes the line d3–g3, so that white can retort 2 KxP dis ck. It also opens the line e5–a1 for the white queen, enabling her to mate by 3 Qa1, when she is unpinned by 2 —— Rf4. This is the most brilliant line of play in the composition, but there are several other variations that are of interest.

66

KENNETH S. HOWARD
American Chess Bulletin
July–August, 1938

White mates in three moves

THE POSSIBILITY OF an en passant pawn capture is much
less apparent in No. 66 than it is in the two preceding
problems. One reason for this is because the capture is
made by white and does not occur until the mating move.
In solving this problem it is likely that the experienced
solver will consider first the pinning of white's knight's
pawn and decide that the thematic play undoubtedly involves unpinning this pawn so it may discover check. Then
the solver will note that black can interpose his king's
bishop's pawn, but that it may be removed by an en passant capture. The complication involving a cross-check
may be somewhat of a surprise.

This problem illustrates the unique feature of a pinned
white pawn discovering check along a diagonal parallel
to the one on which the pawn itself is moving.

67

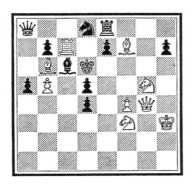

KENNETH S. HOWARD
First Commended
British Chess Magazine
Informal Tourney, July–December,
1941

White mates in three moves

AFTER SOLVING NO. 66, the solver may expect similar strategic effects from the appearance of No. 67. Here again an en passant pawn capture may not be immediately suggested by the initial position, although the solver should always investigate such a possibility when there is a pawn on its home rank with a pawn of opposing color that could make the capture. In solving No. 67 the solver may also remember that in both 65 and 66 en passant pawn captures were blended with cross-checks.

An important feature of No. 67 is the defensive distinction between 1 —— Qc8 and 1 —— Bd7; white's reply to the former not being effective after the latter. Other defenses, particularly 1 —— Pe6, should not be overlooked. This latter move is an *anticipatory interference* on the black queen and bishop, for if 2 —— Qc8 or 2 —— Bd7, the pawn on e6 will interfere with check to the white king.

68

GILBERT DOBBS
First Honorable Mention
American Chess Bulletin
Informal Tourney, 1939

White mates in three moves

IT IS A QUESTION whether No. 68 can be solved more readily by analyzing the construction or by trying to determine the theme. In solving from construction, whenever a direct battery is seen it is a good plan to experiment with the battery checks. Should the solver do this here he soon will conclude that white's king's rook must be moved or be guarded by a second piece. This may lead him to try 1 Kg2. Then he will see that 1 —— Se3 ck leads to the pyrotechnical line, 2 RxS ck, KxR dis ck; 3 Sf3. He may decide that black checks are the theme of the problem, and then may work out the 1 —— Qa2 ck variation, an even more brilliant line because of the pin and unpin of the white knight.

White pawns, because of their limited mobility, often are guideposts to the solution, so problems without white pawns frequently are the more difficult to solve.

69

VINCENT L. EATON
Second Prize
17th International Tourney
Skakbladet, 1937

White mates in three moves

THE SOLVER WILL FIND in No. 69 that two variations are
set, viz., 1 —— Bc5 ck; 2 Kb5 dis ck, Bb4 dis ck; 3 Qd5,
and 1 —— QxS ck; 2 Ka3 dis ck, Qc4; 3 QxQ. These constitute the theme of the problem. In the first variation
there are consecutive black and white checks, the second
checking move of black unpinning the white queen so
that she can mate. In the second variation white changes
the direction of the pin on his queen by moving his king,
and black then unpins the white queen by a withdrawal
move, again allowing her to mate. In effect, this is a doubling of the thematic play.

The key and the threat in this spectacular composition
are not related to the thematic play and for that very reason they may be the more difficult to discover. The key
adds a sparkling subsidiary line to the first variation given
above.

70

VINCENT L. EATON
*Entry in Tourney No. 20
British Chess Federation
1936*

White mates in three moves

THE BLACK KING-BISHOP battery in No. 70 suggests a cross-check theme, but if the black king is to discover check he must be given one or more flight squares. Thus the solver immediately has a good clue to the solution. In contrast to problem 69, the key of No. 70 is definitely thematic, since the keymove makes possible the cross-checks.

Because of the elaborate construction of this composition it may require some time for the solver to work out the continuations, even after the key has been found. Observe that in the two principal variations white self-pins a man on the second move, and black then unpins the same man, permitting it to deliver mate. In addition to these brilliant variations, there is much interesting play in the secondary lines, in one of which there are additional cross-checks.

71

GILBERT DOBBS
British Chess Magazine
July, 1939

White mates in three moves

PROBLEM 71 IS AN EXAMPLE of a position where white seemingly has an unnecessarily large force, and one in which care must be taken not to stalemate black. The veteran solver may recognize this as a type of problem in which one of the white pieces has to be temporarily *masked,* and apparently the only piece that can be shut off, or masked, to any purpose is the king's rook.

This problem illustrates what is known as the *Indian theme,* named after a problem composed a century ago by an English clergyman, Rev. H. A. Loveday, who was living in India. Dr. Dobbs, in No. 71, doubles the thematic play, which is a fine constructive feat considering that he uses but eight men altogether. The square on which the masking occurs is known as a *critical square,* because the rook has to withdraw across it, the withdrawal being a *critical move.*

72

JOHN F. BARRY
The Boston Transcript
April 26, 1932

White mates in three moves

THE NUMEROUS PIECES and complicated setting of No. 72 may make it look more difficult than some of the preceding problems. The main-play of this composition illustrates a striking theme, but there is considerable interesting secondary play. In fact, it might easily be possible for a solver to find the key and work out the secondary variations without even recognizing the main-play. The position of the white queen should suggest that the solver must find a way to bring her into action, probably by clearing the third rank.

The problem was composed by the late Bostonian player, editor and problem critic, as an illustration in three-move form of a two-move theme that was dubbed the *American Indian* by the great Sam Loyd. The thematic play runs, 1 Rf7, BxR; 2 BxS, BxR; 3 BxQ; the last three moves constituting the American Indian theme.

73

WALTER JACOBS
First Prize
American Chess Bulletin
Informal Tourney, 1942

White mates in three moves

NO. 73 IS TYPICAL of many modern three-movers. The solver doubtless will at once note 1 Qh1, threatening 2 Qb1 mate. This is the *thematic try,* but it is defeated by 1 —— Qd5. This try, however, may become an effective continuation if black can be induced to make a move which will prevent the black queen from reaching d5. The solver accordingly should seek a key that will bring about this situation. Actually it is produced by an interference between black pieces of like motion, of a type known as a *Holzhausen interference.*

The variations of this problem also illustrate in three-move form a general defense by black, a white contingent threat and black correction play, which as a two-move feature was explained in connection with problem 34. The key of No. 73 threatens a pretty sacrifice, leading to a mate that is a model, following one of black's moves.

74

WILLIAM B. RICE
First Prize
First C. C. L. A. Tourney, 1936

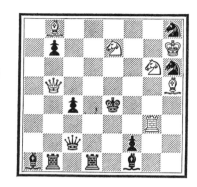

White mates in three moves

THE ARRANGEMENT of the black rooks, bishops and queen in Rice's prize winner suggests a black interference theme. The black rooks and bishops guard four squares from which the white queen can check, viz., b7, c4, d5, and e5. In the actual play she also checks from b1 in one variation. The key is aggressive, threatening a *short mate*, which is a mate in less than the stipulated number of moves.

Any one of several moves of the black queen temporarily defeats the threat. In each case, however, the queen makes a Holzhausen interference with another black piece of like motion, in such a way that she may be decoyed from her station by a sacrificial check by the white queen. In view of this achievement of five distinct Holzhausen interferences by the black queen, the aggressiveness of the key becomes a relatively minor defect.

75

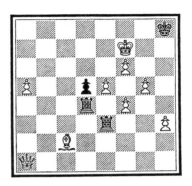

OTTO WURZBURG
V *American Chess Bulletin*
May–June, 1936

White mates in three moves

IN PROBLEM 73 a black bishop interfered with the black queen on a diagonal; while in problem 74 the black queen interfered with each bishop in turn on a diagonal, with each rook on a file, and with one rook on a rank. These interferences were all Holzhausens because they were not mutual. A mutual interference between two black pieces of like motion is termed a *Plachutta interference* when a white man is sacrificed on the interference, or critical, square. When there is no sacrifice it is a *Wurzburg-Plachutta.*

The position of the black rooks in No. 75 suggests mutual interferences on d3 and e4; a move of either rook to either of these squares shutting off the white bishop's guard on h7. Here the Wurzburg-Plachutta interference is doubled, since black has four thematic continuations. Why should black seek to shut off the guard on h7?

76

KENNETH S. HOWARD
The Chess Correspondent
May–June, 1944

White mates in three moves

THE WHITE QUEEN and queen's knight are seemingly out of play in No. 76. Since no queen move looks promising as a key, the knight's possible moves may be scrutinized. 1 Sa2 and 1 Sa5 are obviously useless. 1 Sc2 leads to no mating threat. The drastic 1 SxB actually is defeated only by 1 —— Rd3. This black move may be a clue, suggesting 1 Sd5 to prevent the black rook from reaching d3. After 1 —— Sd5 white threatens 2 Sf4 ck, KSxS; 3 Re3.

Black can capture the knight with rook or bishop, but this produces an interference similar to a Nowotny. Following a capture of the white knight, the white queen makes a checking capture. This forces whichever black piece has captured the knight to open a line that permits the queen to mate. This maneuver is termed a *Brunner-Plachutta,* or by some authorities a *Brunner-Nowotny* interference. The incidental defense 1 —— BxQ should not be overlooked.

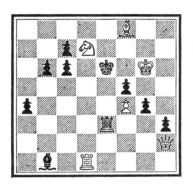

KENNETH S. HOWARD
V British Chess Magazine
July, 1944

White mates in three moves

THE QUEEN IS SO OUT of play in No. 77 that the solver may be inclined to move her at once. 1 Qb2 is tempting, but 1 —— Rd3 or 1 —— Bd3 is an adequate defense. The relation of these black pieces may now suggest that a mutual interference between them on d3 may be the feature of the problem. Accordingly the solver should look for a threat, other than 1 Qb2, to which these moves will be defenses. For instance, these moves might be made by black to prevent the white rook from passing over d3 on white's second move.

The ensuing play resembles that in No. 76. Here, however, no white man is sacrificed on the interference square, and the black interferences are like a Grimshaw rather than a Nowotny. So the maneuver illustrated may be called a *Brunner-Grimshaw*. There is an interesting try, 1 SxP, met only by 1 —— Rb3.

78

RICHARD CHENEY
Third Honorable Mention
American Chess Bulletin
Informal Tourney, 1944

White mates in three moves

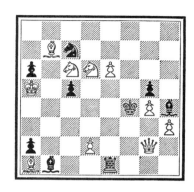

IN EXAMINING NO. 78 the solver will probably soon notice that white's king's bishop is shut out of play by the knight on c6. If the knight were removed, white could mate immediately by Qf3. The veteran solver, however, will realize that perhaps this knight may wait until the second move to release the guard of the bishop on f3. Then an inspection of the black pieces shows that the lines of movement of the queen's bishop and of the rook cross at e4. This suggests that possibly e4 may be the critical square in a mutual Grimshaw interference theme.

In solving the problem it will be found that even if black plays either the rook or bishop across e4 on the first move, these pieces can be forced to interfere so as to enable white to mate. Technically the problem illustrates *multi-phase* Grimshaw mutual interferences.

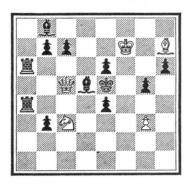

79

WALTER JACOBS
V *First Prize*
American Chess Bulletin
Informal Tourney, 1944

White mates in three moves

THE SETTING OF NO. 79 suggests that the theme probably is based on the interplay of the black pieces. The multiple guarding of squares in the black king's field precludes the possibility of model mates. The key should be easy to find, since in the initial position the knight is not effectively located and there are only two squares that look like advantageous posts. When the knight is moved to one of these the mating threat is obvious.

The interest in the position lies in the defensive maneuvers. Black has two ways of defeating the initial threat. In each case white proceeds with a quiet second move, setting up a new threat. Again black can defeat the threat, but in doing so allows another mate. Black's first defensive moves are *square obstructions* and his second interferences.

80

GEORGE W.
HARGREAVES
First Honorable Mention
American Chess Bulletin
Informal Tourney, 1943

White mates in three moves

ALTHOUGH THE INITIAL POSITION of No. 80 does not suggest any favorable line of attack for white, the very fact that the black king seems so strongly intrenched behind his pawns may lead the solver to try a sacrificial attack on those pawns.

The problem has two thematic valve plays by the black knight affecting the moves of the white queen; these variations originating from moves of the black bishop to b2 and c1 respectively. A *valve* move is a move that interferes with one line of movement of another piece and simultaneously opens a second line for that piece. The key of No. 80 is excellent, interfering with a line of movement of the queen only to open the line again by the second move threat. The keymove also makes the defense 1 —— Bb2 potentially effective. Do not overlook the secondary defenses, 1 —— Sd6 and 1 —— Be7, the latter leading to a block position.

81

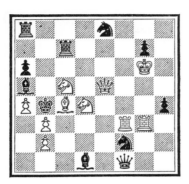

WALTER JACOBS
First Prize
American Chess Bulletin
Informal Tourney, 1941

White mates in three moves

UNTIL THE KEYMOVE is made in No. 81 it may be difficult to recognize the striking theme the problem illustrates. Accordingly the solver may find the key more readily by examining the construction than by attempting in advance to determine the theme. Once the key is discovered, the four thematic variations should not be hard to work out. The theme, which is quadrupled, is line clearance by sacrifices of white pieces.

The key may be found most easily by noting which white piece seems out of play. The second-move threat, however, may not be simple to find even after the key has been made, and a curious feature of the problem is that the threat is actually required only after the most purposeless black moves on the board. In fact, the thematic play might all be worked out without the threat even being noticed.

82

P. L. ROTHENBERG
*V Second Honorable Mention
American Chess Bulletin
Informal Tourney, 1942*

White mates in three moves

HERE AGAIN THE SETTING is not suggestive; the apparently unrelated arrangement of the white pieces in no way revealing the theme. Yet whenever the black king seems particularly well entrenched a sacrificial attack may prove successful, as it did in problem 80. If such an attack is to be made in No. 82, it probably will be by white's king's rook. This may be a sufficient hint to enable the solver to find the key.

The problem was composed to show, in three-move form, two distinct lines of play in each of which a black piece makes a random defense and a correction move. These terms were explained in *Section One* and illustrated in connection with problems 34, 36, 57 and 73. In No. 82 the thematic defenses are made by black's queen's knight and king's bishop, and the problem should not be regarded as solved until such defenses are worked out in detail.

WALTER JACOBS
American Chess Bulletin
September–October, 1942

White mates in three moves

SINCE SIX OF THE SQUARES in the black king's field are guarded only once, it is probable that some of the mates in No. 83 will be models. Then from the location of the black pieces it seems likely that black's principal defenses will be based on moves of the knight on c3.

When the problem is solved it will be found that random moves of the black knight, such as 1 —— Sd1, e2, defeat the initial threat but allow a contingent threat, 2 Qg4 ck, which leads to the model mate, 2 —— Kd5; 3 Pc4. 1 —— Se4 is a correction move, defeating both the initial and contingent threats, but resulting in a second model mate. The key is very obscure, as its only purpose is to make possible white's mating move following the black correction play. This type of problem often is solved most readily by noting what continuations may follow moves of the black pieces.

84

A. J. FINK
American Chess Bulletin
November–December, 1942

White mates in three moves

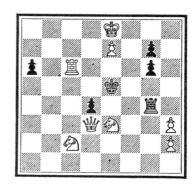

WHEN IT WAS FIRST PUBLISHED NO. 84 puzzled many solvers, probably because white's second-move continuations in two of the variations were not apparent, although the idea had been used previously. In problem 81 the white knights were sacrificed to clear lateral and diagonal lines for the white queen. As a hint to the solver, the theme of No. 84 is *square vacating*, effected by sacrifices. During the solution white moves a piece, not for the purpose of permitting another piece to move across the square on which the first piece stood, but to occupy that particular square; and in the operation the first piece is sacrificed. Fink has embellished the idea by having model mates follow the captures of the sacrificed piece.

This is the kind of problem which probably is most easy to solve by looking for a key that seems to threaten a likely attack.

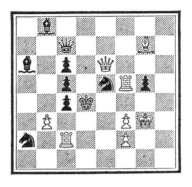

WALTER JACOBS
First Prize
American Chess Bulletin
Informal Tourney, 1943

White mates in three moves

IF NO. 85 WERE A TWO-MOVER, the black queen on a line with the white king would immediately suggest a cross-check theme. Even here the experienced solver may try unpinning the knight by 1 Rf6 to see what will happen, and he will find that a discovered check by black is met by double-check by white, followed by mate.

Black accordingly will not move the knight until forced to do so, but white threatens to make the knight move by 2 Qg4 ck. If 2 — — SxQ ck, then Rd6 mates, the queen having cleared the line f6 – d6 for the rook. Black's defenses lie in making 2 Qg4 ck ineffective, but in each case white is able to force, or *decoy*, the knight to a different square, there being four such decoys altogether, three being by queen sacrifices. The line clearances for the rook here should be compared with those for the queen in problem 81.

86

OTTO WURZBURG
Second Honorable Mention
American Chess Bulletin
Informal Tourney, 1939

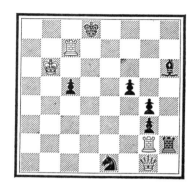

White mates in three moves

IN EXAMINING NO. 86 the solver will see at once that the only way in which black can be mated is by having the white queen or king's rook reach the eighth rank. Accordingly the theme of the problem will probably be based on line openings by black. It is clear that nothing can be gained by moving the white king or queen's rook. Therefore the keymove must be made by the other rook or the queen. Then it soon will be seen that no move of white's king's rook is effective, so that the queen must make the keymove, and she has a choice of eight squares.

This method of solving by the elimination of ineffective moves is particularly serviceable in problems where there are only a few white pieces. Besides the threat line there are five variations, and the subtle defense 1 —— Bg5 should not be overlooked.

87

VINCENT L. EATON
*Second Honorable Mention
American Chess Bulletin
Informal Tourney, 1943*

White mates in three moves

THE SETTING OF NO. 87 may remind the solver of the play in problem 84, since the solver will note that if the white queen vacates a2, the knight threatens mate there. Should the queen move immediately, however, black would capture the knight. The keymove therefore must delay the capture, and with this hint it should readily be discovered.

After the keymove black has several ways to prevent the knight from mating. Three defenses involve captures of white men on the queen's bishop's file. In each case the white queen moves up the rook's file behind the capturing black piece, so if the black piece moves again to defeat 3 Sa2, a diagonal will be opened for the queen to mate on the first rank. Thus the theme is another line-opening one. In this case black removes obstructing white men by capture, or by *annihilation,* as the theme is termed.

88

ERIC M. HASSBERG
*First Commended
American Chess Bulletin
Informal Tourney, 1943*

White mates in three moves

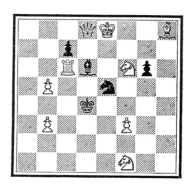

IN EXAMINING NO. 88 it soon will be seen that the black king must not be allowed to escape to e2 via d3. Then, also, 1 —— SxR looks like an unanswerable defense. So this shortly may lead the solver to try 1 Sd5. This is an example of what is termed a *give-and-take* key, for though unpinning the black bishop it pins the knight. If 1 —— KxS, white continues 2 Qg5, and then if 2 —— Ke6; 3 QxS. This is the main-play.

Note the odd pinning and unpinning effects. White's first move pins the black knight and unpins the black bishop. Black's reply again pins the bishop and unpins the knight. White's second move again pins the knight and unpins the bishop. Then black's second move once more reverses the pins. This is an amusing procedure. All other play in the problem is incidental and of no especial interest.

89

VINCENT L. EATON
First Prize
Skakbladet
1936

White mates in three moves

PROBLEM NO. 89 HAS a sophisticated type of theme. The white rooks on the third rank, with the white king and black rook, form a *white half-pin*. While either rook alone may move off the rank, both of them cannot do so unless black makes an unpinning move. Such a move would be a withdrawal of the black rook or an interference on the line of pin, such as 1 —— Pd3 or 1 —— Pc3. This may give a clue to the solution. The solver should look for a keymove leading to a threat against which these pawn moves will be defenses. For each of these moves mates are set, viz., 1 —— Pc3; 2 Re5 ck, KxR; 3 Rf5, and 1 —— Pd3; 2 Rf5 ck, SxR; 3 Re5.

This is a problem where the key may be found most readily by noting which white men must retain their stations; another form of elimination than that used to solve problem 86.

90

VINCENT L. EATON
Third Honorable Mention
(ex aequo)
British Chess Magazine
Informal Tourney, January–June,
1937

White mates in three moves

THE OPENNESS OF THE SETTING, and the fact that all eight white pieces and seven black pieces are employed, make No. 90 look like a difficult problem to solve. On examination, however, the solver will find that the positions of most of the white pieces are fixed, at least for the first move, so the problem is another example of one that is most readily solved by the elimination method. The knight-rook battery is a fixture, and neither white's queen's knight, king nor queen's bishop can move without permitting a disastrous check. The white queen is apparently required where she is for guarding purposes, as is the king's bishop. From this analysis it appears that the queen's rook must make the keymove.

The theme, a white half-pin blended with cross-checks, is disguised by the presence of the black queen on the line of pin.

91

GILBERT DOBBS
First Honorable Mention
Third Cheney Miniature Tourney
1937

White mates in three moves

PROBLEM 91 DOES NOT PROMISE much strategic play. The black rook may pin a white piece, threaten check or block a square in the black king's field, but these are only mildly strategic features. On the other hand, the position is a relatively open one and the black king has a flight-square. So the probability is that this is a model mate problem. The solver who is familiar with the work of prominent composers, often can tell by the name of the composer the kind of composition to expect. The late Dr. Dobbs, for example, specialized in model mate problems.

Actually there are three model mates in No. 91. One occurs in the threat line; a second in a variation where there is a cross-check and where the black rook blocks the black king; and in a third, where the rook again self-blocks.

92

OTTO WURZBURG
American Chess Bulletin
July–August, 1936

White mates in three moves

IN WHAT IS KNOWN as a *mating net* type of model mate problem, black has no actively defensive moves and the composition shows merely a number of model mating positions, often brought about by moves of the black king to different flight-squares. Such problems frequently feature mates by knights and bishops in various combinations.

No. 92 is a borderline example of this type of problem. It has six technically different model mating positions; there being some difference in each of them in the final arrangement of the white pieces or in the square on which the black king is mated. The problem has a slight strategic element, however, in the mutual interference between the black bishop and king's pawn, which is termed a *pawn-Grimshaw*. In a mating net problem the key frequently gives the black king additional flight-squares, which is a solving hint for No. 92.

OTTO WURZBURG
First Prize
American Chess Bulletin
Informal Tourney, 1939

White mates in three moves

IN A THREE-MOVER with flight squares, one method of solving is to look for mates following moves of the black king. In No. 93, when the reply to 1 —— Ke4 is discovered, the continuation will be found so beautiful that the solver will recognize he is on the right track. Then 1 —— Pg5 should be tried. In each case white's second move is a sacrifice, followed by a model mate.

The defenses by the black queen, 1 —— Qd3 and 1 —— Qe4, turn out to be self-blocks, and in both of the ensuing mates a white piece shuts off the line of guard of the black queen. Thus the problem combines two attractive model mating positions with a variety of strategic play. Finally, note the use made of the white rook; in two lines it acts as a guard, in a third it pins a black pawn, and in a fourth it delivers mate.

94

KENNETH S. HOWARD
Commended
The Western Morning News
Informal Tourney, July–December,
1935

White mates in three moves

THE POSITION OF THE WHITE knights in No. 94 suggests possible mates by 3 Sc6 and 3 Sf3, if the black pieces guarding these squares can be decoyed. The queen is apparently the only white piece available to effect these decoys, and to free the queen to move she must be relieved from guarding the bishop on d3. Since the bishop cannot be guarded by any piece other than the queen, the key is probably a withdrawal move by the bishop. This is a logical method of figuring out the keymove.

1 Be2 seems a likely keymove because it also prevents 1 —— Pe2. Now is there a second-move threat? Yes, 2 Qd5 ck, followed by 2 —— RxQ; 3 Sc6, a model mate. The threat can be defeated by 1 —— Pc2 and by 1 —— Re4. These defenses are also met by queen sacrifices, forcing black self-blocks, and leading to model mates. A fourth model mate follows 1 —— Rd8 ck; 2 KxR, Pc2; 3 Qf6.

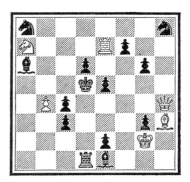

95

WALTER JACOBS
American Chess Bulletin
July–August, 1935

White mates in three moves

THE LOCATIONS OF THE FEW white men in No. 95 make it probable that the key can be determined most readily by elimination and a short analysis will undoubtedly convince the solver that the queen is the most likely man to make the keymove. The greatest difficulty undoubtedly will be in finding the second move continuations. The position of the pawns in the black king's field, however, may remind the solver of the sacrificial methods used in solving problem 80.

The key threatens a mate to which the defenses in three instances result in *anticipatory* self-blocks. In each of these three thematic variations, the man moved on black's first move blocks the black king in the mate. In all three of these variations white's second move is a sacrifice, and two of the variations have model mates. Jacobs frequently succeeds in combining strategic maneuvers with model mates.

96

GILBERT DOBBS
Commended
British Chess Magazine
Informal Tourney, July–December,
1937

White mates in three moves

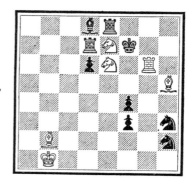

IN PROBLEMS CONSTRUCTED to illustrate model mating positions, echoes of the mates are especially attractive, particularly where the mating positions are complex. When the black king is mated on squares of the same color in each of the echoed mates, it is a *monochrome* echo. To echoes in which the black king is mated on squares of different colors, the picturesque term *chameleon* has been applied. In most instances chameleon echoes are more difficult to construct than are monochrome.

Dr. Dobbs was fond of echoing model mates and No. 96 is an excellent example of his skill. To solve this problem the solver should look for arrangements of the white men that will lead to echoed mating positions. As a hint, the solver may note that there is a move that will place all the white pieces, except the king, in a symmetrical relationship to the black king.

97

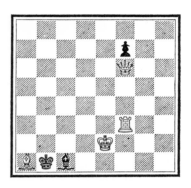

OTTO WURZBURG
First Honorable Mention
American Chess Bulletin
Informal Tourney, 1940

White mates in three moves

OTTO WURZBURG is another famous composer who frequently shows echoed model mates, especially in his miniatures. So the solver naturally will expect such mates in No. 97. This problem has an excellent key, which, however, it should not be too difficult to find because there are not many plausible tries.

The key sets up a waiting move position, which is unusual in a problem of this type. In addition to the monochrome echoed model mates, there is a second pair of echoed mates in which the mating positions are not models. The solver will observe that the mating positions themselves have a symmetrical relation to each other. He should also note how the black pawn prevents dual mates in both model mating lines. It is by observing these niceties of construction that the solver gets the full measure of enjoyment from so artistic a composition.

98

GILBERT DOBBS
American Chess Bulletin
April, 1936

White mates in three moves

IN NO. 98 THE BLACK KING has flight-squares at f4 and f6, which apparently will lead to considerable freedom on the knight's file. So a natural move for white would be 1 Rf2, cutting off these flights and giving in exchange the single flight-square d6. If 1 —— Kd6, 2 Sd3 confines the king to the eighth rank. 2 —— Pc5 is followed by 3 Rf6 mate, but black can play 2 —— Ke6 instead. Now white could mate if the rook could reach g6 or h6. From these experimental moves the solution should soon be found.

The variations in this problem are further examples of symmetrical play, followed by echoed model mates. In each of the two model mating positions, in which the black king stands either on e6 or f5, there are no men in the black king's field, the king being surrounded by vacant squares. Such mates are known as *mirror mates*.

OTTO WURZBURG
Second Commended
American Chess Bulletin
Informal Tourney, 1943

White mates in three moves

IN THE INITIAL POSITION in No. 99 the white men are arranged symmetrically in relation to the black king. Frequently a problem of this kind can be solved by seeking a keymove that does not disturb the symmetry. This is not always the case, however, since in some instances the key may be what is termed an *asymmetric* one. Where the symmetrical arrangement is vertical, as in No. 99, there will be more files on one side of the *axis of symmetry* than on the other, and sometimes a key may be based on this feature.

In this problem it will be noticed that the black men are not symmetrically arranged, and when the solution has been worked out the solver will see how important it is that the white queen can reach a1. The problem has two pairs of symmetrically echoed model mates.

100

OTTO WURZBURG
*Second Honorable Mention
American Chess Bulletin
Informal Tourney, 1944*

White mates in three moves

THE DISCERNING SOLVER may recognize the possibility of a symmetrical arrangement of the white pieces in relation to the black king in No. 100 and select a move for the key which will bring about such an arrangement. After doing this the four second-move continuations will readily be found. Of course white cannot play 1 Sf3, because it releases the black rook to check the white king.

The echoing play in this problem lies in white's second moves, which make a quadruple echo, and this is the feature of the composition. The bishop and the black rook are essential to make the mechanism work, and there necessarily are duals on the mating moves. Wurzburg has composed many lightweight three-movers in which the white rooks play a major role, and attractive examples of these have already been seen in problems 59 and 60.

101

WALTER JACOBS
First Prize
American Chess Bulletin
Informal Tourney, 1940

White mates in three moves

BLACK HAS SUCH a great variety of defensive play in Jacobs' prize-winner that the solver at first may wonder where to begin in his attempt to unravel the solution. Probably the best line to follow will be to endeavor to find a mating continuation after the flight capture, 1 — — KxP. Undoubtedly the most difficult feature of the solution is white's second-move threat, which was the kernel of the composer's idea when he started to construct the problem.

When the problem is completely solved it will be found that its content includes six model mating positions, two of which are echoes, and also two queen sacrifices. During the course of the solution white's king's knight plays to seven different squares. The solver should not feel that he has mastered this remarkable composition until he has worked out in detail all the variations.

102

KENNETH S. HOWARD
2d and 3rd Honorable Mention
(ex aequo)
The Western Morning News
Informal Tourney, January–June,
1936

White mates in three moves

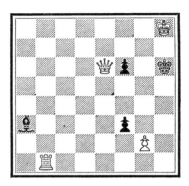

ALTHOUGH IN NO. 102 the white queen, pawn and rook are all some distance from the black king, the rook appears the most out of play and so is probably the man that makes the keymove. It next is a question onto which square to move him. In a problem of such light weight it is likely that there is at least one model mate. So the solver should endeavor to visualize a possible model mating position. The black bishop will be found to be very effective in preventing cooks.

In the complete solution it will be discovered that there are two model mating positions, in both of which the white queen, pawn and rook stand in the same relation to the black king, but in one variation the king is mated on a white square and in the second on a black one. This constitutes a chameleon echo.

103

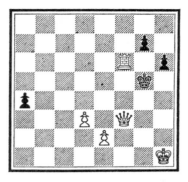

KENNETH S. HOWARD
American Chess Bulletin
March–April, 1944

White mates in three moves

THE SETTING OF NO. 103 suggests a model mate problem, possibly showing echoed mates. It is apparent that white cannot allow the rook to be captured, so the key must be a rook move. To withdraw an attacked piece to a safer position is not a meritorious type of key, but sometimes a composer is unable to provide a better one.

If the rook is withdrawn along the rank it will retain its guard on g6, and while no particular square may seem indicated, the experienced solver will be inclined to move it to the a-file, attacking the pawn on a4. Now it will be seen that after 1 —— Pa3, a random move, 2 Ra5ck leads to a model mate, the black king being self-blocked by his pawn. If 1 —— Pg6, white continues 2 RxPa4, showing the purpose of 1 Ra6. This variation leads to a chameleon echo of the preceding mate.

104

WILLIAM B. RICE
The Emery Memorial
1937

White mates in three moves

NO. 104 IS A NOTABLE composition, featuring chameleon echoed pairs of pin-mates, one of the most difficult types of problems to compose. In each of the four thematic mates a black piece is necessarily pinned, and in each pair the mates are symmetrical. None of the mates is a model, since the required arrangement of the white knights leads to the double guarding of one square in each mate, but this is a minor matter. What will appeal most to the solver is the geometrical accuracy of the play, and the fact that it is produced in so economical a setting.

The key is not too apparent, although in a position of this kind the solver will do well to experiment by endeavoring to set up a somewhat symmetrical arrangement of the white pieces. He can, at least, secure a symmetrical relationship of the knights to the rooks.

ONLY A relatively small number of four-move problems are composed in these days. Formerly many problems were composed to be solved in four or more moves that actually only embodied a three-move theme, an extra move or two being added merely to perplex the solver.

According to today's standards of composition, no more moves should be employed than are necessary to express the problemistic idea the composer desires to illustrate. This limits the modern four-mover to ideas that cannot be fully carried out in three moves, or at least not expressed so well. No. 105 is an illustration of this latter point. Although the idea of No. 105 could be shown in three moves, the use of the additional move enhances the illustration of the idea and makes the problem more pleasing. In such a model mate composition as No. 109, four moves are required to bring about the echoed mating positions.

The usual four-move problem often is easier to solve than a complex three-mover. Because of the great constructional difficulties involved, only a few outstanding composers have the technical skill and patience to construct elaborate four-movers with several complex variations. So ordinarily the four-move problem is either a dainty miniature or a strategic composition designed to illustrate some strikingly thematic line of play, which may not be complicated with secondary variations.

In general, the same methods of solving used for three-movers may be applied to four-movers. It usually is easy to determine from the setting of a four-mover whether it is a strategic or a model mate problem, and this knowledge will greatly aid the solver in working out the solution.

For instance, a problem where the black force is limited to king and pawns, and perhaps a single minor black piece, is probably one composed primarily for its mating positions. Likewise a composition with a relatively open setting and with the squares around the black king only singly guarded, or blocked, should lead the solver to expect a model mate problem. If the black king has one or more flights, it is even more likely that the problem was composed to show model mates.

The pleasure in solving this type of problem lies, to a large extent, in noting the beauty of the mating positions. So no model mate problem should be regarded as really solved until all the model mates in it have been fully worked out.

Frequently a model mate problem can be solved most readily by envisaging the possible model mating positions, and then deciding what move as a key will be required to make the mechanism operate. Sometimes model mate problems have very fine keys, difficult to discover. In many cases, on the other hand, the key is a merely perfunctory move, which is employed solely to secure a sound setting.

A problem composed primarily to illustrate some strategic maneuver can commonly be distinguished in any one of several ways. The position may be relatively more complex than is usual in a model mate problem. The squares around the black king may have so many unnecessary guards that the solver will see at a glance that model mates cannot occur. Perhaps just the general arrangement of the men will suggest to the experienced solver the strategic theme the composer designed the problem to illustrate.

105

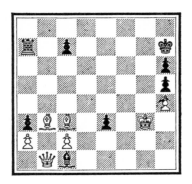

WALTER JACOBS
American Chess Bulletin
January, 1936

White mates in **four moves**

JACOBS' 105 IS A BRILLIANT example of a four-mover with a single thematic line. The solver will see that black can check on his second move with rook or bishop, if not forced to give immediate attention to some threat by white. Then the sequestered location of the white queen suggests that her surroundings must be opened up in some way so she can take part in the play. These considerations at once limit the possible white moves to be examined. Once the correct keymove is tried, the continuations will be relatively easy to find.

Ordinarily a threat of mate in fewer moves than the number stipulated is regarded as a defect. In this particular problem, however, the threat of immediate mate that occurs after both white's first and second move is not such a defect, since the threats are an inherent part of the theme.

106

A L A I N   W H I T E   *and*
O T T O   W U R Z B U R G
American Chess Bulletin
March–April, 1944

White mates in four moves

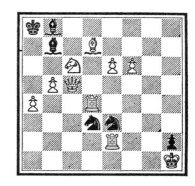

THE KEY OF NO. 106 is an aggressive one and the problem should prove fairly easy to solve. After the keymove neither black bishop can move without mate following immediately. One, or the other, of the black knights makes a defensive move and white captures it. The remaining knight has eight squares to which it may move, but white, on his third move, captures the black knight wherever it goes. This leaves black in a complete block position, or *zugzwang*, forcing him to move one of the bishops.

A problem where one or more black men are captured to produce such a block position illustrates the *grab theme*, of which this composition is an elaborate example. Since the eight squares on which one knight is captured are all black and the eight on which the other knight is captured are white, the combined grab play has a chameleon effect.

107

GILBERT DOBBS
American Chess Bulletin
March–April, 1942

White mates in four moves

AFTER DR. DOBBS' DEATH in 1941 this beautiful four-mover was found among his unpublished compositions. It is a type of problem that should not be hard to solve once the solver notices the nearly symmetrical arrangement of the men. Symmetry has already been discussed in connection with problems 96, 97, 99 and 100. In No. 107 the key completes the symmetry of the position and sets up a waiting-move situation. Yet the continuations may require some study, since all white's second and third moves are quiet, a term applied to moves that are not checks or captures, as explained in *Section One*.

The lines of play are echoed throughout and they terminate in two pairs of echoed mates, the mates in one pair being models. The odd black pawn on e7 stops a second solution by 1 Qf7, while the white king is placed so as to prevent a solution by 1 Qh1 ck.

108

GILBERT DOBBS
Fifth Commended
Third Cheney Miniature Tourney
1937

White mates in four moves

THIS PROBLEM HAS an inviting appearance, but the solver soon will discover that it lacks the guideposts he might find in a position which had more men. Perhaps the readiest way to solve a problem of this kind is to experiment by moving the black king, and then attempt to visualize possible mating positions.

Since Dr. Dobbs was fond of echoed mates, when the solver has found one line that leads to a mate in four moves, he should see if he cannot find an echo of the mate in another line. The problem has such echoes, although the mates are not models. In both main lines white's third moves may be difficult to find. When the sixteen honored problems in this tourney were published in the *American Chess Bulletin*, one of the *Bulletin's* most skillful solvers stated that he found this problem the most difficult of the sixteen.

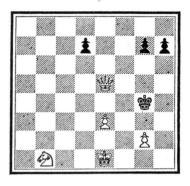

109

KENNETH S. HOWARD
American Chess Bulletin
February, 1936

White mates in four moves

THE SETTING OF NO. 109 suggests a model mate problem, since black has no pieces to make any strategical defense, nor can white produce much strategical play with only a queen and a knight. The knight is obviously so out of play that it probably makes the keymove. Actually the composer was obliged to place the knight so far from the field of action to avoid second solutions.

If the solver notices that the setting of this problem has some resemblance to that of No. 102, he may expect to find chameleon echoed model mates here also, and his chief task will be to work out the model mating positions. In addition to a pair of echoed models, there is a second pair of echoed chameleon mates which are not models, and these should not be overlooked for they add considerably to the interest of the composition.

110

KENNETH S. HOWARD
First Prize
Second Cheney Miniature Tourney
1936

White mates in four moves

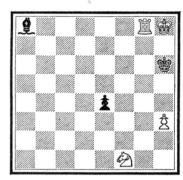

NO. 110 IS ANOTHER PROBLEM where the setting suggests that it was composed to show chameleon echoed model mates, and it is apparent that the rook is the only man which can be utilized to give the actual mates. Next it will be seen that the knight will have to be employed to guard squares on the rook's file adjacent to the black king. This leaves to the white pawn the duty of supporting the rook in the mating positions. So much can be figured out merely by examining the initial position.

The model mates in this problem, like those in Nos. 97, 99, 102, and 109, are termed *side-of-board models* in distinction from models where the black king is away from the side of the board. Side-of-board models usually are easier to construct than are models where it is necessary to guard eight squares around the black king.

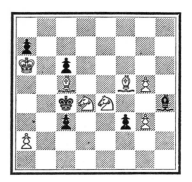

MAXWELL BUKOFZER
The Emery Memorial
1937

White mates in four moves

MAXWELL BUKOFZER has specialized in model mate problems in which the white men, besides king and pawns, are restricted to bishops and knights, and No. 111 is one of his finest compositions of this character. Similarly to the four previous problems, No. 111 is of the so-called mating net type, in which black has no strategic defensive play and the solver's task is merely to set up a series of mating positions. No. 111 may be found considerably more difficult than some of the preceding problems because of its greater complexity. Perhaps the best method to employ in solving it is the one suggested in connection with problem 108.

There is a threatened mate in three moves, which, however, may not be readily seen. The feature of the composition is a pair of model mates that form an attractive chameleon echo, and there are three other model mates in addition.

112

OTTO WURZBURG
First Prize
Third Cheney Miniature Tourney
1937

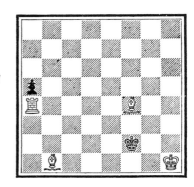

White mates in four moves

THIS IS ONE of the most beautiful miniatures ever composed. The author was the judge in the Third Cheney Tourney and in his award commented on this position as follows: "This beautiful composition has two pairs of chameleon echo model mates and a third chameleon echo of impure mates. While the mating positions themselves are familiar ones I have never seen them shown as chameleon echoes. The problem is a constructive masterpiece. The point of the key is accentuated by a close try; there are no checks in any of the continuations; and each of the four white pieces is active in the course of the solution, the rook and each bishop giving mate in turn."

Here again there are no guideposts to the solution, outside of the apparent fact that the black king must not be allowed to escape to g4.

Solutions

NO. 1	*1* Ra2
NO. 2	*1* Bh5
NO. 3	*1* Qc1
NO. 4	*1* Sd7
NO. 5	*1* Ra8
NO. 6	*1* Bg8
NO. 7	*1* Sd4
NO. 8	*1* Be4
NO. 9	*1* Bg5
NO.10	*1* Sc1
NO.11	*1* Kc4
NO.12	*1* Re7
NO.13	*1* Rf3
NO.14	*1* Qa5
NO.15	*1* Pc6
NO.16	*1* QxP
NO.17	*1* Qh3
NO.18	*1* Pb5
NO.19	*1* Pd5
NO.20	*1* Sd6

NO.21	*1* Se4
NO.22	*1* Qg3
NO.23	*1* Qc7
NO.24	*1* Kc2
NO.25	*1* Qa5
NO.26	*1* Rb3
NO.27	*1* Ba3
NO.28	*1* Ba4
NO.29	*1* Bh5
NO.30	*1* Sg5
NO.31	*1* Sf5
NO.32	*1* Sc1
NO.33	*1* Qg7
NO.34	*1* Bh1
NO.35	*1* Sd3
NO.36	*1* Ke7
NO.37	*1* Qg4
NO.38	*1* Bh6
NO.39	*1* QSd3

NO.40	*1* Pe4
NO.41	*1* Re4
NO.42	*1* QRe5
NO.43	*1* Bg1
NO.44	*1* Qc3
NO.45	*1* Qg8
NO.46	*1* Bb8
NO.47	*1* Qb1
NO.48	*1* Qb1
NO.49	*1* Pe6
NO.50	*1* Sf6
NO.51	*1* Qc7
NO.52	*1* Sc8
NO.53	*1* Rb5
NO.54	*1* Sa4
NO.55	*1* Se5
NO.56	*1* Rf7
NO.57	*1* Pd4
NO.58	*1* Qh1

NO.59
1 Ra2, Qc7, h2; *2* Ra8 ck
      Qc8, g8; *2* Rh2 ck

NO.60

1 Rc6, *threat* 2 QxP ck, QRxQ; 3 RxRP
                              KRxQ; 3 Rc8
                              KxQ; 3 RxBP
            PxR; 2 QxP ck
            Pb6 ck; 2 RxSP ck

NO.61

1 Qc3, Kc8; 2 Qc5, K any; 3 Pc8=Q
   Ke8; 2 Qe5, K any; 3 Pe8=Q

NO.62

1 Pa8=B, Kf1; 2 BxP; Ke2; 3 Bd3
   Pe3; 2 Bg2, PxB; 3 Re5

NO.63

1 Qf6, *threat* 2 Bd3, any;   3 Qd6
   Ke4; 2 Bc4, Pe2;   3 Qf4
   Kc5; 2 Qc6 ck, Kb4; 3 Bc3
   Sf3; 2 Qd6 ck, Ke4; 3 Bd3

NO.64

1 Pd4, *threat* 2 Pd5 ck, PxP; 3 BxP
   BPxPep; 2 Qa2 ck, Pd5; 3 BPxPep
   KPxPep; 2 Pf4, *threat*   3 Pf5
                     Pf5; 3 PxPep
   Pd5; 2 BxPc6

NO.65

1 Pe4, *threat* 2 Kg4 ck
   PxPep ck; 2 KxSP ck, Rf4; 3 Qa1
   Rf3 ck; 2 KxR
   RxP; 2 KxP ck

NO.66

1 Pc6, *threat* 2 Re8 ck
   Qe7 ck; 2 Pg5 ck, Pf5; 3 PxPep
   Qd6; 2 Re8 ck, Kd5; 3 Re5
   QxB; 2 Re8 ck, Kf6; 3 RxPf7
   QxP ck; 2 BxQ ck

NO.67

1 Qg3, Qc8 ck; 2 Pf5 ck (*threat*), Pe5; 3 PxPep
   Bd7 ck; 2 Be6, *threat*   3 Pf5
                     SxB; 3 Sf7
   Pe6; 2 SxPd4, any;   3 Qa3
   Pe5; 2 PxP ck

NO.68
1 Kg2, *threat* 2 QS any, mate
  Qa2 ck; 2 Se2 ck, QxR;   3 Sg3
  Se3 ck; 2 RxS ck, KxR ck; 3 Sf3

NO.69
1 Ba6, *threat* 2 Se2 ck, KxS;   3 Bd3
  Bc5 ck; 2 Kb5 ck, Bb4 ck; 3 Qd5
              Kd3;   3 Kc6
  QxS ck; 2 Ka3 ck, Qb4 ck; 3 RxQ

NO.70
1 Sc8–d6, *threat* 2 QxB ck
    KxR ck; 2 Sf7 ck, Ke6;   3 Sd8
    Ke5 ck; 2 Pf7 ck, Ke6;   3 Pf8=S
    Qe8; 2 SxP ck, KxR ck; 3 Sd6–f7
              Ke5 ck;   3 Sd6–f7

NO.71
1 Rh1, Kg4; 2 Kh2, Kh5; 3 Kg3
    Pg4; 2 Sh2, Kh4; 3 Sf1

NO.72
1 Rf7, RxR ck; 2 Rf4 ck (*threat*)
    BxR; 2 BxS, *threat*   3 Qb3
          BxR;   3 BxQ

NO.73
1 Qh6, Pf4; 2 QxP ck (*threat*), RxQ; 3 SxP
    Bh5, h7; 2 Qc6 ck, Qd5;   3 QxQ
    Bf7; 2 Qh1, any;   3 Qb1

NO.74
1 Ba7, *threat* 2 Re3 mate
    Qb3; 2 QxPb7 ck, QxQ; 3 Re3
    Qc1; 2 QxR ck
    Qc3; 2 Qe5 ck
    Qd2; 2 Qd5 ck
    Qe2; 2 QxPc4 ck

NO.75
1 Pg6, *threat* 2 Pg7 mate
    Rd4–d3; 2 Qa3, RxQ; 3 Pg7
    Re3–d3; 2 Qd1
    Rd4–e4; 2 Qa4
    Re3–e4; 2 Qe1

NO.76
1 Sd5, *threat* 2 Sf4 ck, KSxS; 3 Re3
    BxS; 2 QxP ck, Bc4; 3 Qh5
    RxS; 2 QxS ck, Re5; 3 Qa2
    BxQ; 2 KxS, *threat*   3 Re3
                  Sf4 ck; 3 SxS

NO.77
1 Sf6, *threat* 2 Rd8, any;   3 Re8
    Bd3; 2 Qa2 ck, Bc4; 3 QxB
    Rd3; 2 Qe2 ck, Re3; 3 Qc4

NO.78
1 Sc4, *threat* 2 Se7, Be4; 3 Be5
               Re4; 3 Sg6
    Bf5–h7; 2 Sb4, Be4; 3 Be5
               Re4; 3 Sd3
    RxP; 2 Sd4, Be4; 3 Se2

NO.79
1 Sb5, *threat* 2 Qc3 ck
    Rc4; 2 Qe7, *threat* 3 Qf6
               Bc6; 3 QxPe6
    Rc6; 2 Qf2, *threat* 3 Qf6
               Bc4; 3 Qd4

NO.80
1 Rf7, *threat* 2 RxP ck, KxR; 3 Qh5
    Bb2; 2 Qb8 ck, Sd6; 3 QxKB

NO.81
1 Rg5, *threat* 2 BxQ, *threat*   3 Qe1
            Sd3; 2 Sc2 ck, BxS;   3 Qc3
            Se4; 2 Sd3 ck, QxS;   3 QxB
            Sd6; 2 Sc6 ck, RxS;   3 Qc3
            Bb6; 2 SxP ck, RxS;   3 Qb5

NO.82
1 Qg8, *threat* 2 RxS ck, PxR;   3 Qc8
         SxS, d2; 2 Rb5 ck, PxR;   3 Qc8
            Sd4; 2 Sd3 ck, Kc4;   3 Sa3
         Bc1–h6; 2 Pd8–S, any;   3 Sb7
         Bf6–d8; 2 Qg1 ck, Sd4;   3 QxS
            Bh4; 2 Qg4, *threat*   3 Qc4
               QS any;   3 Qd4

NO.83
1 Kg2, *threat* 2 Qd3
   QS any (except e4); 2 Qg4 ck, Kd5; 3 Pc4
               Se4; 2 Qb3 ck, Kf5; 3 Qh3

NO.84
1 Se1, *threat* 2 Sf3 ck
            Re4; 2 Qb5 ck, PxQ;   3 Sd3
            Rf4; 2 Qe4 ck, KxQ;   3 Re6

NO.85
1 Rf6, *threat* 2 Qg4 ck, SxQ ck;   3 Rd6
            Bc8; 2 QxPc4 ck, SxQ ck;   3 Rd6
            Qd7; 2 QxQ ck, SxQ ck;   3 Rd6
            Sc3; 2 Rd2 ck, Sd3 ck;   3 Rf4

NO.86
1 Qh1, *threat* 2 Rd2 ck, RxR;   3 Qa8
            SxR; 2 Qa1, any;   3 Qa8
            RxR; 2 Qh4 ck, Bg5;   3 Qh8
            RxQ; 2 Ra2, any;   3 Ra8
            Ke8; 2 Re2 ck, any;   3 Qa8
            Bg5; 2 RxR

NO.87

1 Rc5, SxP; 2 Qa8, *threat* 3 Sa2
                     SxS; 3 Qh1
     BxR; 2 Qa7, BxS; 3 Qg1
     BxP; 2 Qa6, BxP; 3 Qf1
     Re3; 2 Qa5
     QxP; 2 Qa3
     RxSP; 2 QxR
     RxBP; 2 Qa6

NO.88

1 Sd5, *threats* 2 Sb4, Sf4
        KxS; 2 Qg5, Ke6; 3 QxS

NO.89

1 Qc8, *threat* 2 Sc7 ck
        Pc3; 2 Re5 ck, KxR; 3 Rf5
        Pd3; 2 Rf5 ck, SxR; 3 Re5

NO.90

1 Rb1, *threat* Re1 ck
              Qc4 ck; 2 Sd5 ck, Se7; 3 Sd6
              Qf4 ck; 2 Sf5 ck, Se7; 3 Sc5
              QxS ck; 2 RxQ ck

NO.91

1 Kb8, Rg6; 2 Sd7–f6 ck (*threat*), RxS; 3 Qe7
       Kf7 ck; 2 Sf8 ck, KxS;   3 Qe7
       Rg7; 2 Qc8 ck, Kf7;   3 Se5

NO.92

1 Se5, *threat* 2 Sd7 ck, Ka5; 3 Be1
        Ka5; 2 Be1 ck, Kb6; 3 Sd7
        Kc5; 2 Sd3 ck, Kb6; 3 Bc7
        Pe6; 2 KSc4 ck, Kc5; 3 Bd6
        Pd3; 2 Bf2 ck, Ka5; 3 Sc6
        Be6; 2 Sd3, Ka5;   3 Bc7

NO.93

1 Qb6, *threat* 2 Sf2 ck, Kg5;   3 Qd8
          Ke4; 2 Qe3 ck, PxQ;   3 Sg4–e5
          Pg5; 2 Qg6 ck, KxQ;   3 Sg4–e5
          Qd3; 2 Se3 ck, Ke4;   3 Bg2
          Qe4; 2 Sg4–e5 ck, Kg5; 3 Qd8

NO.94

1 Be2, *threat* 2 Qd5 ck, RxQ; 3 Sc6
          Pc2; 2 Qc5 ck, SxQ; 3 Bb2
          Re4; 2 QxR ck, SxQ; 3 Sf3
      Rd8 ck; 2 KxR, Pc2;   3 Qf6

NO.95

1 Qf6, *threat* 2 Qf3 ck
          Pe4; 2 Qe5 ck, PxQ;   3 Rd7
          Rd3; 2 QxQP ck, KxQ; 3 Rd7
          Rd4; 2 RxKP ck, PxR; 3 Qc6

NO.96

1 Sf8, *threat* 2 Rg7 ck
          KxSf8; 2 Rg8 ck, KxS;   3 RxR
          KxSe7; 2 Re6 ck, KxS;   3 RxR
          RxSf8; 2 Rg1 ck, K any; 3 Re1
          RxSe7; 2 Rh6 ck, K any; 3 Rh8

NO.97

1 Rf5, Ka2; 2 Ra5 ck, Kb1; 3 Qf5
                      Ba3; 3 Qb2
          Ba3; 2 Rf1 ck, Ka2; 3 QxP
                      Bc1; 3 Qb2
          Kc2; 2 Rb5

NO.98

1 Rg2, Kd6; 2 Sd3, Ke6; 3 Rg6
      Kf4, f6; 2 Sc4, Kf5; 3 Rf7

NO.99

1 Ke4, *threat*	2 Qg3 ck, Kd1;	3 Sg4–e3	
Rg1;	2 Qc3 ck, Kf1;	3 Sc4–e3	
Kc1;	2 Sg4–e3 ck, Ke1;	3 Qg3	
Kf1;	2 Sc4–e3 ck, Ke1;	3 Qc3	

NO.100

1 Sa5, Kc5; 2 Rd7
       Ke5; 2 Rd3
       Kd4; 2 Rf5
       Kd6; 2 Rb5

NO.101

1 Qf4, Ra1; 2 Bb4 (*threat*), KxP; 3 Sc3
      Pd5; 2 Bb4 (*threat*), KxP; 3 Sd6
      Ra4; 2 Sc3 ck, KxSc5; 3 SxR
      Sa6; 2 Sf6 ck, KxS; 3 SxP
      KxP; 2 Sf6 ck, KxS; 3 Qb4
      Bh2; 2 QxP ck, KxQ; 3 Bf2
  Sb6, e7; 2 Qe5 ck, KxQ; 3 Bc3

NO.102

1 Rg1, Bc1, c5, d6; 2 QxP ck (*threat*), Kh5; 3 Pg4
           Kh5; 2 Qf5 ck, Kh4; 3 Pg3
        K else; 2 PxP ck (*threat*)

NO.103

1 Ra6, Pa3; 2 Ra5 ck, Kg6; 3 Qf5
      Pg6; 2 RxPa4, Ph5; 3 Qf4
      Kh4; 2 Rg6, *threat* 3 Qg4
             Ph5; 3 Qg3
    Ph5; 2 Qg3 ck, Kf5; 3 Pe4

NO.104

1 Sf5–d6, Kd5; 2 Rh5 ck (*threat*), Be5; 3 Sc3
                       Qe5; 3 Sf6
         Qg8; 2 Ra5 ck (*threat*), Bd5; 3 Sc4
                       Qd5; 3 Sf7

NO.105
1 Bf6, Kg6; 2 Be5, Kf5; 3 Bd4, Ke4; 4 Pc3

NO.106
1 Qb6, *threat* 2 Qa5 ck
          Sc4; 2 RxSc4, S any; 3 RxS
        Sf2 ck; 2 RxSf2
          Sc5; 2 RxS
          Sb4; 2 Bc8

NO.107
1 Qd1, KxBP; 2 Qb1, Kd5; 3 Qe1, Kc5; 4 Qa5
                                 Pc5; 4 Qe4
        KxKP; 2 Qf1, Kd5; 3 Qc1, Ke5; 4 Qg5
                                 Pe5; 4 Qc4

NO.108
1 QxP, Kd4; 2 QxP ck, Ke5; 3 Qd2, Kf5; 4 Qg5
        Pd2; 2 Qd6 ck, Kc4; 3 Qd7, Kb4; 4 Qa4
        Kc4; 2 Qd6
        Kc6; 2 Qd6 ck

NO.109
1 Sd2, Ph6; 2 Se4 (*threat*), Pd6; 3 Sf2 ck, Kh4; 4 Pg3
                              Pg5; 3 Sf6 ck, Kh4; 4 Qh2
        Pd6; 2 Qe6 ck, Kh5;   3 Sf3, *threat*   4 Pg4
                                            Pg6; 4 Qh3

NO.110
1 Se3, *threat* 2 Sf5 ck, Kh5; 3 Ph4, any;   4 Rg5
          Kh5; 2 Sg2, B any; 3 Sf4 ck, Kh4; 4 Rg4
                                        Kh6; 4 Rg6
        Bd5; 2 SxB, Kh5;   3 Sf4 ck

NO.111
1 Sc2, *threat* 2 Sb4
          Kd3; 2 Sf2 ck, Kd2; 3 Be3 ck, Ke2; 4 Bd3
                          Ke2; 3 Bd3 ck, Kd2; 4 Be3
                          Kc4; 3 Sd3, Kd5;   4 Se3
          Kd5; 2 Se3 ck, Ke5; 3 Sf2, BxPg3;   4 Sd3
                                   BxPg5; 4 Sg4

NO.112

1 Bf5, Kf1; *2* Bg4, Kf2; *3* Bd2, Kg3; *4* Be1
                                         Kf1; *4* Rf4
        Kf3; *2* Kg1, Ke2; *3* Bc2, Kf3; *4* Bd1
                                        Ke1; *4* Re4
        Ke2; *2* Kg2, Ke1; *3* Bd3, Kd1; *4* Ra1
        Ke1; *2* Kg2, Ke2; *3* Bc2, Ke1; *4* Re4

Index of Composers

General Index

Unprovided flight, 51, 94
Unprovided flight-capture, 52, 53

V

Vacation, square, 7, 126
Valve, 122
Variation, 17
  secondary, 17
  thematic, 17

W

Waiting move, 8
Waiting move problem, 35
White half-pin, 131, 132
Withdrawal unpin, 63, 64, 65
Wurzburg-Plachutta interference,
  117

CATALOGUE OF DOVER BOOKS

Chess, Checkers, Games, Go

THE ADVENTURE OF CHESS, Edward Lasker. A lively history of chess, from its ancient beginnings in the Indian 4-handed game of Chaturanga, through to the great players of our day, as told by one of America's finest masters. He introduces such unusual sidelights and amusing oddities as Maelzel's chess-playing automaton that beat Napoleon 3 times. Major discussion of chess-playing machines and personal memories of Nimzovich, Capablanca, etc. 5-page chess primer. 11 illustrations, 53 diagrams. 296pp. 5⅜ x 8.   S510 Paperbound **$1.75**

A TREASURY OF CHESS LORE, edited by Fred Reinfeld. A delightful collection of anecdotes, short stories, aphorisms by and about the masters, poems, accounts of games and tournaments, photography. Hundreds of humorous, pithy, satirical, wise, and historical episodes, comments, and word portraits. A fascinating "must" for chess players; revealing and perhaps seductive to those who wonder what their friends see in the game. 48 photographs (14 full page plates) 12 diagrams. xi + 306pp. 5⅜ x 8.   T458 Paperbound **$1.75**

HOW DO YOU PLAY CHESS? by Fred Reinfeld. A prominent expert covers every basic rule of chess for the beginner in 86 questions and answers: moves, powers of pieces, rationale behind moves, how to play forcefully, history of chess, and much more. Bibliography of chess publications. 11 board diagrams. 48 pages.   **FREE**

THE PLEASURES OF CHESS, Assiac. Internationally known British writer, influential chess columnist, writes wittily about wide variety of chess subjects: Anderssen's "Immortal Game;" only game in which both opponents resigned at once; psychological tactics of Reshevsky, Lasker; varieties played by masters for relaxation, such as "losing chess;" sacrificial orgies; etc. These anecdotes, witty observations will give you fresh appreciation of game. 43 problems. 150 diagrams. 139pp. 5⅜ x 8.   T597 Paperbound **$1.25**

WIN AT CHESS, F. Reinfeld. 300 practical chess situations from actual tournament play to sharpen your chess eye and test your skill. Traps, sacrifices, mates, winning combinations, subtle exchanges, show you how to WIN AT CHESS. Short notes and tables of solutions and alternative moves help you evaluate your progress. Learn to think ahead playing the "crucial moments" of historic games. 300 diagrams. Notes and solutions. Formerly titled CHESS QUIZ. vi + 120pp. 5⅜ x 8.   T438 Paperbound **$1.00**

THE ART OF CHESS, James Mason. An unabridged reprinting of the latest revised edition of the most famous general study of chess ever written. Also included, a complete supplement by Fred Reinfeld, "How Do You Play Chess?", invaluable to beginners for its lively question and answer method. Mason, an early 20th century master, teaches the beginning and intermediate player more than 90 openings, middle game, end game, how to see more moves ahead, to plan purposefully, attack, sacrifice, defend, exchange, and govern general strategy. Supplement. 448 diagrams. 1947 Reinfeld-Bernstein text. Bibliography. xvi + 340pp. 5⅜ x 8.   T463 Paperbound **$2.00**

THE PRINCIPLES OF CHESS, James Mason. This "great chess classic" (N. Y. Times) is a general study covering all aspects of the game: basic forces, resistance, obstruction, opposition, relative values, mating, typical end game situations, combinations, much more. The last section discusses openings, with 50 games illustrating modern master play of Rubinstein, Spielmann, Lasker, Capablanca, etc., selected and annotated by Fred Reinfeld. Will improve the game of any intermediate-skilled player, but is so forceful and lucid that an absolute beginner might use it to become an accomplished player. 1946 Reinfeld edition. 166 diagrams. 378pp. 5⅜ x 8.   T646 Paperbound **$1.85**

LASKER'S MANUAL OF CHESS, Dr. Emanuel Lasker. Probably the greatest chess player of modern times, Dr. Emanuel Lasker held the world championship 28 years, independent of passing schools or fashions. This unmatched study of the game, chiefly for intermediate to skilled players, analyzes basic methods, combinations, position play, the aesthetics of chess, dozens of different openings, etc., with constant reference to great modern games. Contains a brilliant exposition of Steinitz's important theories. Introduction by Fred Reinfeld. Tables of Lasker's tournament record. 3 indices. 308 diagrams. 1 photograph. xxx + 349pp. 5⅜ x 8.   T640 Paperbound **$2.25**

THE ART OF CHESS COMBINATION, E. Znosko-Borovsky. Proves that combinations, perhaps the most aesthetically satisfying, successful technique in chess, can be an integral part of your game, instead of a haphazard occurrence. Games of Capablanca, Rubinstein, Nimzovich, Bird, etc. grouped according to common features, perceptively analyzed to show that every combination begins in certain simple ideas. Will help you to plan many moves ahead. Technical terms almost completely avoided. "In the teaching of chess he may claim to have no superior," P. W. Sergeant. Introduction. Exercises. Solutions. Index. 223pp. 5⅜ x 8.   T583 Paperbound **$1.60**

MODERN IDEAS IN CHESS, Richard Reti. An enduring classic, because of its unrivalled explanation of the way master chess had developed in the past hundred years. Reti, who was an outstanding theoretician and player, explains each advance in chess by concentrating on the games of the single master most closely associated with it: Morphy, Anderssen, Steinitz, Lasker, Alekhine, other world champions. Play the games in this volume, study Reti's perceptive observations, and have a living picture of the road chess has travelled. Introduction. 34 diagrams. 192pp. 5⅜ x 8.   T638 Paperbound **$1.25**

THE BOOK OF THE NEW YORK INTERNATIONAL CHESS TOURNAMENT, 1924, annotated by A. Alekhine and edited by H. Helms. Long a rare collector's item, this is the book of one of the most brilliant tournaments of all time, during which Capablanca, Lasker, Alekhine, Reti, and others immeasurably enriched chess theory in a thrilling contest. All 110 games played, with Alekhine's unusually penetrating notes. 15 photographs. xi + 271pp. 5⅜ x 8.
T752 Paperbound **$1.85**

KERES' BEST GAMES OF CHESS, selected, annotated by F. Reinfeld. 90 best games, 1931-1948, by one of boldest, most exciting players of modern chess. Games against Alekhine, Bogolyubov, Capablanca, Euwe, Fine, Reshevsky, other masters, show his treatments of openings such as Giuoco Piano, Alekhine Defense, Queen's Gambit Declined; attacks, sacrifices, alternative methods. Preface by Keres gives personal glimpses, evaluations of rivals. 110 diagrams. 272pp. 5⅜ x 8.   T593 Paperbound **$1.35**

HYPERMODERN CHESS as developed in the games of its greatest exponent, ARON NIMZOVICH, edited by Fred Reinfeld. An intensely original player and analyst, Nimzovich's extraordinary approaches startled and often angered the chess world. This volume, designed for the average player, shows in his victories over Alekhine, Lasker, Marshall, Rubinstein, Spielmann, and others, how his iconoclastic methods infused new life into the game. Use Nimzovich to invigorate your play and startle opponents. Introduction. Indices of players and openings. 180 diagrams. viii + 220pp. 5⅜ x 8.   T448 Paperbound **$1.50**

THE DEVELOPMENT OF A CHESS GENIUS: 100 INSTRUCTIVE GAMES OF ALEKHINE, F. Reinfeld. 100 games of the chess giant's formative years, 1905-1914, from age 13 to maturity, each annotated and commented upon by Fred Reinfeld. Included are matches against Bogolyubov, Capablanca, Tarrasch, and many others. You see the growth of an inexperienced genius into one of the greatest players of all time. Many of these games have never appeared before in book form. "One of America's most significant contributions to the chess world," Chess Life. New introduction. Index of players, openings. 204 illustrations. xv +227pp. 5¾ x 8.
T551 Paperbound **$1.35**

RESHEVSKY'S BEST GAMES OF CHESS, Samuel Reshevsky. One time 4-year-old chess genius, 5-time winner U. S. Chess Championship, selects, annotates 110 of his best games, illustrating theories, favorite methods of play against Capablanca, Alekhine, Bogolyubov, Kashdan, Vidmar, Botvinnik, others. Clear, non-technical style. Personal impressions of opponents, autobiographical material, tournament match record. Formerly "Reshevsky on Chess." 309 diagrams, 2 photos. 288pp. 5⅜ x 8.   T606 Paperbound **$1.25**

ONE HUNDRED SELECTED GAMES, Mikhail Botvinnik. Author's own choice of his best games before becoming World Champion in 1948, beginning with first big tournament, the USSR Championship, 1927. Shows his great power of analysis as he annotates these games, giving strategy, technique against Alekhine, Capablanca, Euwe, Keres, Reshevsky, Smyslov, Vidmar, many others. Discusses his career, methods of play, system of training. 6 studies of endgame positions. 221 diagrams. 272pp. 5⅜ x 8.   T620 Paperbound **$1.50**

RUBINSTEIN'S CHESS MASTERPIECES, selected, annotated by Hans Kmoch. Thoroughgoing mastery of opening, middle game; faultless technique in endgame, particularly rook and pawn endings; ability to switch from careful positional play to daring combinations; all distinguish the play of Rubinstein. 100 best games, against Janowski, Nimzowitch, Tarrasch, Vidmar, Capablanca, other greats, carefully annotated, will improve your game rapidly. Biographical introduction, B. F. Winkelman. 103 diagrams. 192pp. 5⅜ x 8.
T617 Paperbound **$1.25**

TARRASCH'S BEST GAMES OF CHESS, selected & annotated by Fred Reinfeld. First definitive collection of games by Siegbert Tarrasch, winner of 7 international tournaments, and the leading theorist of classical chess. 183 games cover fifty years of play against Mason, Mieses, Paulsen, Teichmann, Pillsbury, Janwoski, others. Reinfeld includes Tarrasch's own analyses of many of these games. A careful study and replaying of the games will give you a sound understanding of classical methods, and many hours of enjoyment. Introduction. Indexes. 183 diagrams. xxiv + 386pp. 5⅜ x 8.   T644 Paperbound **$2.00**

MARSHALL'S BEST GAMES OF CHESS, F. J. Marshall. Grandmaster, U. S. Champion for 27 years, tells story of career; presents magnificent collection of 140 of best games, annotated by himself. Games against Alekhine, Capablanca, Emanuel Lasker, Janowski, Rubinstein, Pillsbury, etc. Special section analyzes openings such as King's Gambit, Ruy Lopez, Alekhine's Defense, Giuoco Piano, others. A study of Marshall's brilliant offensives, slashing attacks, extraordinary sacrifices, will rapidly improve your game. Formerly "My Fifty Years of Chess." Introduction. 19 diagrams. 13 photos. 250pp. 5⅜ x 8.   T604 Paperbound **$1.45**

THE HASTINGS CHESS TOURNAMENT, 1895, edited by Horace F. Cheshire. This is the complete tournament book of the famous Hastings 1895 tournament. One of the most exciting tournaments ever to take place, it evoked the finest play from such players as Dr. Lasker, Steinitz, Tarrasch, Harry Pillsbury, Mason, Tchigorin, Schlecter, and others. It was not only extremely exciting as an event, it also created first-rate chess. This book contains fully annotated all 230 games, full information about the playing events, biographies of the players, and much other material that makes it a chess classic. 22 photos, 174 diagrams. x + 370pp. 5⅜ x 8½.
T288 Paperbound **$2.00**

THE BOOK OF THE NOTTINGHAM INTERNATIONAL CHESS TOURNAMENT, 1936, Annotated by Dr. Alexander Alekhine. The Nottingham 1936 tournament is regarded by many chess enthusiasts as the greatest tournament of recent years. It brought together all the living former world champions, the current chess champion, and the future world champion: Dr. Lasker, Capablanca, Alekhine, Euwe, Botvinnik, and Reshevsky, Fine, Flohr, Tartakover, Vidmar, and Bogoljubov. The play was brilliant throughout. This volume contains all 105 of the games played, provided with the remarkable annotations of Alekhine. 1 illustration, 121 diagrams. xx + 291pp. 5⅜ x 8½.
T189 Paperbound **$2.00**

CHESS FOR FUN AND CHESS FOR BLOOD, Edward Lasker. A genial, informative book by one of century's leading masters. Incisive comments on chess as a form of art and recreation, on how a master prepares for and plays a tournament. Best of all is author's move-by-move analysis of his game with Dr. Emanuel Lasker in 1924 World Tournament, a charming and thorough recreation of one of the great games in history: the author's mental processes; how his calculations were upset; how both players blundered; the surprising outcome. Who could not profit from this study-in-depth? For the enthusiast who likes to read about chess as well as play it. Corrected (1942) edition. Preface contains 8 letters to author about the fun of chess. 95 illustrations by Maximilian Mopp. 224pp. 5⅜ x 8½.
T146 Paperbound **$1.25**

HOW NOT TO PLAY CHESS, Eugene A. Znosko-Borovsky. Sticking to a few well-chosen examples and explaining every step along the way, an outstanding chess expositor shows how to avoid playing a hit-or-miss game and instead develop general plans of action based on positional analysis: weak and strong squares, the notion of the controlled square, how to seize control of open lines, weak points in the pawn structure, and so on. Definition and illustration of typical chess mistakes plus 20 problems (from master games) added by Fred Reinfeld for the 1949 edition and a number of good-to-memorize tips make this a lucid book that can teach in a few hours what might otherwise take years to learn. 119pp. 5⅜ x 8.
T920 Paperbound **$1.00**

THE SOVIET SCHOOL OF CHESS, A. Kotov and M. Yudovich. 128 master games, most unavailable elsewhere, by 51 outstanding players, including Botvinnik, Keres, Smyslov, Tal, against players like Capablanca, Euwe, Reshevsky. All carefully annotated, analyzed. Valuable biographical information about each player, early history of Russian chess, careers and contributions of Chigorin and Alekhine, development of Soviet school from 1920 to present with full over-all study of main features of its games, history of Russian chess literature. The most comprehensive work on Russian chess ever printed, the richest single sourcebook for up-to-date Russian theory and strategy. New introduction. Appendix of Russian Grandmasters, Masters, Master Composers. Two indexes (Players,. Games). 30 photographs. 182 diagrams. vi + 390pp. 5⅜ x 8.
T26 Paperbound **$2.00**

THE ART OF THE CHECKMATE, Georges Renaud and Victor Kahn. Two former national chess champions of France examine 127 games, identify 23 kinds of mate, and show the rationale for each. These include Legal's pseudo sacrifice, the double check, the smothered mate, Greco's mate, Morphy's mate, the mate of two bishops, two knights, many, many more. Analysis of ideas, not memorization problems. Review quizzes with answers help readers gauge progress. 80 quiz examples and solutions. 299 diagrams. vi + 208pp.
T106 Paperbound **$1.35**

HOW TO SOLVE CHESS PROBLEMS, K. S. Howard. Full of practical suggestions for the fan or the beginner—who knows only the moves of the chessmen. Contains preliminary section and 58 two-move, 46 three-move, and 8 four-move problems composed by 27 outstanding American problem creators in the last 30 years. Explanation of all terms and exhaustive index. "Just what is wanted for the student," Brian Harley. 112 problems, solutions. vi +171pp. 5⅜ x 8.
T748 Paperbound **$1.00**

CHESS STRATEGY, Edward Lasker. Keres, Fine, and other great players have acknowledged their debt to this book, which has taught just about the whole modern school how to play forcefully and intelligently. Covers fundamentals, general strategic principles, middle and end game, objects of attack, etc. Includes 48 dramatic games from master tournaments, all fully analyzed. "Best textbook I know in English," J. R. Capablanca. New introduction by author. Table of openings. Index. 167 illustrations. vii + 282pp. 5⅜ x 8.
T528 Paperbound **$1.65**

REINFELD ON THE END GAME IN CHESS, F. Reinfeld. Formerly titled PRACTICAL END-GAME PLAY, this book contains clear, simple analyses of 62 end games by such masters as Alekhine, Tarrasch, Marshall, Morphy, Capablanca, and many others. Primary emphasis is on the general principles of transition from middle play to end play. This book is unusual in analyzing weak or incorrect moves to show how error occurs and how to avoid it. Covers king and pawn, minor piece, queen endings, weak squares, centralization, tempo moves, and many other vital factors. 62 diagrams. vi + 177pp. 5⅜ x 8.
T417 Paperbound **$1.25**

CATALOGUE OF DOVER BOOKS

THE AMERICAN TWO-MOVE CHESS PROBLEM, Kenneth S. Howard. One of this country's foremost contemporary problem composers selects an interesting, diversified collection of the best two-movers by 58 top American composers. Involving complete blocks, mutates, line openings and closings, other unusual moves, these problems will help almost any player improve his strategic approach. Probably has no equal for all around artistic excellence, surprising keymoves, interesting strategy. Includes 30-page history of development of American two-mover from Loyd, its founder, to the present. Index of composers. vii + 99pp. 5⅜ x 8½.
T997 Paperbound **$1.00**

WIN AT CHECKERS, M. Hopper. (Formerly CHECKERS). The former World's Unrestricted Checker Champion discusses the principles cf the game, expert's shots and traps, problems for the beginner, standard openings, locating your best move, the end game, opening "blitzkrieg" moves, ways to draw when you are behind your opponent, etc. More than 100 detailed questions and answers anticipate your problems. Appendix. 75 problems with solutions and diagrams. Index. 79 figures. xi + 107pp. 5⅜ x 8.
T363 Paperbound **$1.00**

GAMES ANCIENT AND ORIENTAL, AND HOW TO PLAY THEM, E. Falkener. A connoisseur's selection of exciting and different games: Oriental varieties of chess, with unusual pieces and moves (including Japanese shogi); the original pachisi; go; reconstructions of lost Roman and Egyptian games; and many more. Full rules and sample games. Now play at home the games that have entertained millions, not on a fad basis, but for millennia. 345 illustrations and figures. iv + 366pp. 5⅜ x 8.
T739 Paperbound **$2.00**

GO AND GO-MOKU, Edward Lasker. A fascinating Oriental game, Go, is winning new devotees in America daily. Rules that you can learn in a few minutes—a wealth of combinations that makes it more profound than chess! This is an easily followed step-by-step explanation of this 2000-year-old game, beginning with fundamentals. New chapter on advanced strategy in this edition! Also contains rules for Go-Moku, a very easy sister game. 72 diagrams. xix + 215pp. 5⅜ x 8.
T613 Paperbound **$1.50**

HOW TO FORCE CHECKMATE, F. Reinfeld. Formerly titled CHALLENGE TO CHESSPLAYERS, this is an invaluable collection of 300 lightning strokes selected from actual masters' play, which will demonstrate how to smash your opponent's game with strong decisive moves. No board needed — clear, practical diagrams and easy-to-understand solutions. Learn to plan up to three moves ahead and play a superior end game. 300 diagrams. 111pp. 5⅜ x 8.
T439 Paperbound **$1.25**

CHESSBOARD MAGIC! A COLLECTION OF 160 BRILLIANT ENDINGS, I. Chernev. Contains 160 endgame compositions, all illustrating not only ingenuity of composition, but inherent beauty of solution. In one, five Knights are needed to force mate; in another White forces stalemate though Black finishes eight passed pawns ahead; 150 more, all remarkable, all will sharpen your imagination and increase your skill. "Inexhaustible source of entertainment, an endless feast of delight," Reuben Fine, Grandmaster. Introduction. 160 diagrams. Index of composers. vii + 172pp. 5⅜ x 8.
T607 Paperbound **$1.00**

LEARN CHESS FROM THE MASTERS, F. Reinfeld. Formerly titled CHESS BY YOURSELF, this book contains 10 games which you play against such masters as Marshall, Bronstein, Najdorf, and others, and an easy system for grading each move you make against a variety of other possible moves. Detailed annotations reveal the principles of the game through actual play. 91 diagrams. viii + 144pp. 5⅜ x 8.
T362 Paperbound **$1.00**

MORPHY'S GAMES OF CHESS, edited by Philip W. Sergeant. You can put boldness into your game by following the brilliant, forceful moves of the man who has been called the greatest chess player of all time. Here are 300 of Morphy's best games carefully annotated to reveal Morphy's principles. 54 classics against masters like Anderssen, Harrwitz, Bird, Paulsen, and others. 52 games at odds; 54 blindfold games; plus over 100 others. Unabridged reissue of the latest revised edition. Bibliography. New introduction by Fred Reinfeld. Annotations and introduction by Sergeant. Index. 235 diagrams. x + 352pp. 5⅜ x 8. T386 Paperbound **$1.85**

CHESS PRAXIS, Aron Nimzovich. Nimzovich was the stormy petrel of chess in the first decades of this century, and his system, known as hypermodern chess, revolutionized all play since his time. Casting aside the classical chess theory of Steinitz and Tarrasch, he created his own analysis of chess, considering dynamic patterns as they emerge during play. This is the fullest exposition of his ideas, and it is easily one of the dozen greatest books ever written on chess. Nimzovich illustrates each of his principles with at least two games, and shows how he applied his concepts successfully in games against such masters as Alekhine, Tarrasch, Reti, Rubinstein, Capablanca, Spielmann and others. Indispensable to every serious chess player. Translated by J. DuMont. 135 diagrams, 1 photo. xi + 364pp. 5½ x 8⅝.
T296 Paperbound **$2.25**

CHESS AND CHECKERS: THE WAY TO MASTERSHIP, Edward Lasker. Complete, lucid instructions for the beginner—and valuable suggestions for the advanced player! For both games the great master and teacher presents fundamentals, elementary tactics, and steps toward becoming a superior player. He concentrates on general principles rather than a mass of rules, comprehension rather than brute memory. Historical introduction. 118 diagrams. xiv + 167pp. 5⅜ x 8.
T657 Paperbound **$1.15**

Puzzles, Mathematical Recreations

SYMBOLIC LOGIC and THE GAME OF LOGIC, Lewis Carroll. "Symbolic Logic" is not concerned with modern symbolic logic, but is instead a collection of over 380 problems posed with charm and imagination, using the syllogism, and a fascinating diagrammatic method of drawing conclusions. In "The Game of Logic" Carroll's whimsical imagination devises a logical game played with 2 diagrams and counters (included) to manipulate hundreds of tricky syllogisms. The final section, "Hit or Miss" is a lagniappe of 101 additional puzzles in the delightful Carroll manner. Until this reprint edition, both of these books were rarities costing up to $15 each. Symbolic Logic: Index. xxxi + 199pp. The Game of Logic: 96pp. 2 vols. bound as one. 5⅜ x 8.
T492 Paperbound **$1.50**

PILLOW PROBLEMS and A TANGLED TALE, Lewis Carroll. One of the rarest of all Carroll's works, "Pillow Problems" contains 72 original math puzzles, all typically ingenious. Particularly fascinating are Carroll's answers which remain exactly as he thought them out, reflecting his actual mental process. The problems in "A Tangled Tale" are in story form, originally appearing as a monthly magazine serial. Carroll not only gives the solutions, but uses answers sent in by readers to discuss wrong approaches and misleading paths, and grades them for insight. Both of these books were rarities until this edition, "Pillow Problems" costing up to $25, and "A Tangled Tale" $15. Pillow Problems: Preface and Introduction by Lewis Carroll. xx + 109pp. A Tangled Tale: 6 illustrations. 152pp. Two vols. bound as one. 5⅜ x 8.
T493 Paperbound **$1.50**

AMUSEMENTS IN MATHEMATICS, Henry Ernest Dudeney. The foremost British originator of mathematical puzzles is always intriguing, witty, and paradoxical in this classic, one of the largest collections of mathematical amusements. More than 430 puzzles, problems, and paradoxes. Mazes and games, problems on number manipulation, unicursal and other route problems, puzzles on measuring, weighing, packing, age, kinship, chessboards, joiners', crossing river, plane figure dissection, and many others. Solutions. More than 450 illustrations. vii + 258pp. 5⅜ x 8.
T473 Paperbound **$1.25**

THE CANTERBURY PUZZLES, Henry Dudeney. Chaucer's pilgrims set one another problems in story form. Also Adventures of the Puzzle Club, the Strange Escape of the King's Jester, the Monks of Riddlewell, the Squire's Christmas Puzzle Party, and others. All puzzles are original, based on dissecting plane figures, arithmetic, algebra, elementary calculus and other branches of mathematics, and purely logical ingenuity. "The limit of ingenuity and intricacy," The Observer. Over 110 puzzles. Full Solutions. 150 illustrations. vii + 225pp. 5⅜ x 8.
T474 Paperbound **$1.25**

MATHEMATICAL EXCURSIONS, H. A. Merrill. Even if you hardly remember your high school math, you'll enjoy the 90 stimulating problems contained in this book and you will come to understand a great many mathematical principles with surprisingly little effort. Many useful shortcuts and diversions not generally known are included: division by inspection, Russian peasant multiplication, memory systems for pi, building odd and even magic squares, square roots by geometry, dyadic systems, and many more. Solutions to difficult problems. 50 illustrations. 145pp. 5⅜ x 8.
T350 Paperbound **$1.00**

MAGIC SQUARES AND CUBES, W. S. Andrews. Only book-length treatment in English, a thorough non-technical description and analysis. Here are nasik, overlapping, pandiagonal, serrated squares; magic circles, cubes, spheres, rhombuses. Try your hand at 4-dimensional magical figures! Much unusual folklore and tradition included. High school algebra is sufficient. 754 diagrams and illustrations. viii + 419pp. 5⅜ x 8.
T658 Paperbound **$1.85**

CALIBAN'S PROBLEM BOOK: MATHEMATICAL, INFERENTIAL AND CRYPTOGRAPHIC PUZZLES, H. Phillips (Caliban), S. T. Shovelton, G. S. Marshall. 105 ingenious problems by the greatest living creator of puzzles based on logic and inference. Rigorous, modern, piquant; reflecting their author's unusual personality, these intermediate and advanced puzzles all involve the ability to reason clearly through complex situations; some call for mathematical knowledge, ranging from algebra to number theory. Solutions. xi + 180pp. 5⅜ x 8.
T736 Paperbound **$1.25**

MATHEMATICAL PUZZLES FOR BEGINNERS AND ENTHUSIASTS, G. Mott-Smith. 188 mathematical puzzles based on algebra, dissection of plane figures, permutations, and probability, that will test and improve your powers of inference and interpretation. The Odic Force, The Spider's Cousin, Ellipse Drawing, theory and strategy of card and board games like tit-tat-toe, go moku, salvo, and many others. 100 pages of detailed mathematical explanations. Appendix of primes, square roots, etc. 135 illustrations. 2nd revised edition. 248pp. 5⅜ x 8.
T198 Paperbound **$1.00**

MATHEMAGIC, MAGIC PUZZLES, AND GAMES WITH NUMBERS, R. V. Heath. More than 60 new puzzles and stunts based on the properties of numbers. Easy techniques for multiplying large numbers mentally, revealing hidden numbers magically, finding the date of any day in any year, and dozens more. Over 30 pages devoted to magic squares, triangles, cubes, circles, etc. Edited by J. S. Meyer. 76 illustrations. 128pp. 5⅜ x 8.
T110 Paperbound **$1.00**

MATHEMATICAL RECREATIONS, M. Kraitchik. One of the most thorough compilations of unusual mathematical problems for beginners and advanced mathematicians. Historical problems from Greek, Medieval, Arabic, Hindu sources. 50 pages devoted to pastimes derived from figurate numbers, Mersenne numbers, Fermat numbers, primes and probability. 40 pages of magic, Euler, Latin, panmagic squares. 25 new positional and permutational games of permanent value: fairy chess, latruncles, reversi, jinx, ruma, lasca, tricolor, tetrachrome, etc. Complete rigorous solutions. Revised second edition. 181 illustrations. 333pp. 5⅜ x 8.
T163 Paperbound **$1.75**

MATHEMATICAL PUZZLES OF SAM LOYD, selected and edited by M. Gardner. Choice puzzles by the greatest American puzzle creator and innovator. Selected from his famous collection, "Cyclopedia of Puzzles," they retain the unique style and historical flavor of the originals. There are posers based on arithmetic, algebra, probability, game theory, route tracing, topology, counter, sliding block, operations research, geometrical dissection. Includes the famous "14-15" puzzle which was a national craze, and his "Horse of a Different Color" which sold millions of copies. 117 of his most ingenious puzzles in all, 120 line drawings and diagrams. Solutions. Selected references. xx + 167pp. 5⅜ x 8. T498 Paperbound **$1.00**

MATHEMATICAL PUZZLES OF SAM LOYD, Vol. II, selected and edited by Martin Gardner. The outstanding 2nd selection from the great American innovator's "Cyclopedia of Puzzles": speed and distance problems, clock problems, plane and solid geometry, calculus problems, etc. Analytical table of contents that groups the puzzles according to the type of mathematics necessary to solve them. 166 puzzles, 150 original line drawings and diagrams. Selected references. xiv + 177pp. 5⅜ x 8. T709 Paperbound **$1.00**

ARITHMETICAL EXCURSIONS: AN ENRICHMENT OF ELEMENTARY MATHEMATICS, H. Bowers and J. Bowers. A lively and lighthearted collection of facts and entertainments for anyone who enjoys manipulating numbers or solving arithmetical puzzles: methods of arithmetic never taught in school, little-known facts about the most simple numbers, and clear explanations of more sophisticated topics; mysteries and folklore of numbers, the "Hin-dog-abic" number system, etc. First publication. Index. 529 numbered problems and diversions, all with answers. Bibliography. 60 figures. xiv + 320pp. 5⅜ x 8. T770 Paperbound **$1.65**

CRYPTANALYSIS, H. F. Gaines. Formerly entitled ELEMENTARY CRYPTANALYSIS, this introductory-intermediate level text is the best book in print on cryptograms and their solution. It covers all major techniques of the past, and contains much that is not generally known except to experts. Full details about concealment, substitution, and transposition ciphers; periodic mixed alphabets, multafid, Kasiski and Vigenere methods, Ohaver patterns, Playfair, and scores of other topics. 6 language letter and word frequency appendix. 167 problems, now furnished with solutions. Index. 173 figures. vi + 230pp. 5⅜ x 8.
T97 Paperbound **$2.00**

CRYPTOGRAPHY, L. D. Smith. An excellent introductory work on ciphers and their solution, the history of secret writing, and actual methods and problems in such techniques as transposition and substitution. Appendices describe the enciphering of Japanese, the Baconian biliteral cipher, and contain frequency tables and a bibliography for further study. Over 150 problems with solutions. 160pp. 5⅜ x 8. T247 Paperbound **$1.00**

PUZZLE QUIZ AND STUNT FUN, J. Meyer. The solution to party doldrums. 238 challenging puzzles, stunts and tricks. Mathematical puzzles like The Clever Carpenter, Atom Bomb; mysteries and deductions like The Bridge of Sighs, The Nine Pearls, Dog Logic; observation puzzles like Cigarette Smokers, Telephone Dial; over 200 others including magic squares, tongue twisters, puns, anagrams, and many others. All problems solved fully. 250pp. 5⅜ x 8.
T337 Paperbound **$1.00**

101 PUZZLES IN THOUGHT AND LOGIC, C. R. Wylie, Jr. Brand new problems you need no special knowledge to solve! Take the kinks out of your mental "muscles" and enjoy solving murder problems, the detection of lying fishermen, the logical identification of color by a blindman, and dozens more. Introduction with simplified explanation of general scientific method and puzzle solving. 128pp. 5⅜ x 8. T367 Paperbound **$1.00**

MY BEST PROBLEMS IN MATHEMATICS, Hubert Phillips ("Caliban"). Only elementary mathematics needed to solve these 100 witty, catchy problems by a master problem creator. Problems on the odds in cards and dice, problems in geometry, algebra, permutations, even problems that require no math at all—just a logical mind, clear thinking. Solutions completely worked out. If you enjoy mysteries, alerting your perceptive powers and exercising your detective's eye, you'll find these cryptic puzzles a challenging delight. Original 1961 publication. 100 puzzles, solutions. x + 107pp. 5⅝ x 8. T91 Paperbound **$1.00**

MY BEST PUZZLES IN LOGIC AND REASONING, Hubert Phillips ("Caliban"). A new collection of 100 inferential and logical puzzles chosen from the best that have appeared in England, available for first time in U.S. By the most endlessly resourceful puzzle creator now living. All data presented are both necessary and sufficient to allow a single unambiguous answer. No special knowledge is required for problems ranging from relatively simple to completely original one-of-a-kinds. Guaranteed to please beginners and experts of all ages. Original publication. 100 puzzles, full solutions. x + 107pp. 5⅜ x 8. T119 Paperbound **$1.00**

Trubner Colloquial Manuals

These unusual books are members of the famous Trubner series of colloquial manuals. They have been written to provide adults with a sound colloquial knowledge of a foreign language, and are suited for either class use or self-study. Each book is a complete course in itself, with progressive, easy to follow lessons. Phonetics, grammar, and syntax are covered, while hundreds of phrases and idioms, reading texts, exercises, and vocabulary are included. These books are unusual in being neither skimpy nor overdetailed in grammatical matters, and in presenting up-to-date, colloquial, and practical phrase material. Bilingual presentation is stressed, to make thorough self-study easier for the reader.

COLLOQUIAL HINDUSTANI, A. H. Harley, formerly Nizam's Reader in Urdu, U. of London. 30 pages on phonetics and scripts (devanagari & Arabic-Persian) are followed by 29 lessons, including material on English and Arabic-Persian influences. Key to all exercises. Vocabulary. 5 x 7½. 147pp.
Clothbound **$1.75**

COLLOQUIAL PERSIAN, L. P. Elwell-Sutton. Best introduction to modern Persian, with 90 page grammatical section followed by conversations, 35-page vocabulary. 139pp.
Clothbound **$1.75**

COLLOQUIAL ARABIC, DeLacy O'Leary. Foremost Islamic scholar covers language of Egypt, Syria, Palestine, & Northern Arabia. Extremely clear coverage of complex Arabic verbs & noun plurals; also cultural aspects of language. Vocabulary. xviii + 192pp. 5 x 7½.
Clothbound **$2.50**

COLLOQUIAL GERMAN, P. F. Doring. Intensive thorough coverage of grammar in easily-followed form. Excellent for brush-up, with hundreds of colloquial phrases. 34 pages of bilingual texts. 224pp. 5 x 7½.
Clothbound **$1.75**

COLLOQUIAL SPANISH, W. R. Patterson. Castilian grammar and colloquial language, loaded with bilingual phrases and colloquialisms. Excellent for review or self-study. 164pp. 5 x 7½.
Clothbound **$1.75**

COLLOQUIAL FRENCH, W. R. Patterson. 16th revision of this extremely popular manual. Grammar explained with model clarity, and hundreds of useful expressions and phrases; exercises, reading texts, etc. Appendixes of new and useful words and phrases. 223pp. 5 x 7½.
Clothbound **$1.75**

COLLOQUIAL CZECH, J. Schwarz, former headmaster of Lingua Institute, Prague. Full easily followed coverage of grammar, hundreds of immediately useable phrases, texts. Perhaps the best Czech grammar in print. "An absolutely successful textbook," JOURNAL OF CZECHO-SLOVAK FORCES IN GREAT BRITAIN. 252pp. 5 x 7½.
Clothbound **$3.00**

COLLOQUIAL RUMANIAN, G. Nandris, Professor of University of London. Extremely thorough coverage of phonetics, grammar, syntax; also included 70-page reader, and 70-page vocabulary. Probably the best grammar for this increasingly important language. 340pp. 5 x 7½.
Clothbound **$2.50**

COLLOQUIAL ITALIAN, A. L. Hayward. Excellent self-study course in grammar, vocabulary, idioms, and reading. Easy progressive lessons will give a good working knowledge of Italian in the shortest possible time. 5 x 7½.
Clothbound **$1.75**

COLLOQUIAL TURKISH, Yusuf Mardin. Very clear, thorough introduction to leading cultural and economic language of Near East. Begins with pronunciation and statement of vowel harmony, then 36 lessons present grammar, graded vocabulary, useful phrases, dialogues, reading, exercises. Key to exercises at rear. Turkish-English vocabulary. All in Roman alphabet. x + 288pp. 4¾ x 7¼.
Clothbound **$4.00**

DUTCH-ENGLISH AND ENGLISH-DUTCH DICTIONARY, F. G. Renier. For travel, literary, scientific or business Dutch, you will find this the most convenient, practical and comprehensive dictionary on the market. More than 60,000 entries, shades of meaning, colloquialisms, idioms, compounds and technical terms. Dutch and English strong and irregular verbs. This is the only dictionary in its size and price range that indicates the gender of nouns. New orthography. xvii + 571pp. 5½ x 6¼.
T224 Clothbound **$2.75**

LEARN DUTCH, F. G. Renier. This book is the most satisfactory and most easily used grammar of modern Dutch. The student is gradually led from simple lessons in pronunciation, through translation from and into Dutch, and finally to a mastery of spoken and written Dutch. Grammatical principles are clearly explained while a useful, practical vocabulary is introduced in easy exercises and readings. It is used and recommended by the Fulbright Committee in the Netherlands. Phonetic appendices. Over 1200 exercises; Dutch-English, English-Dutch vocabularies. 181pp. 4¼ x 7¼.
T441 Clothbound **$2.25**

INVITATION TO GERMAN POETRY record. Spoken by Lotte Lenya. Edited by Gustave Mathieu, Guy Stern. 42 poems of Walther von der Vogelweide, Goethe, Hölderlin, Heine, Hofmannsthal, George, Werfel, Brecht, other great poets from 13th to middle of 20th century, spoken with superb artistry. Use this set to improve your diction, build vocabulary, improve aural comprehension, learn German literary history, as well as for sheer delight in listening. 165-page book contains full German text of each poem; English translations; biographical, critical information on each poet; textual information; portraits of each poet, many never before available in this country. 1 12″ 33⅓ record; 165-page book; album.   The set **$4.95**

ESSENTIALS OF RUSSIAN record, A von Gronicka, H. Bates-Yakobson. 50 minutes of spoken Russian based on leading grammar will improve comprehension, pronunciation, increase vocabulary painlessly. Complete aural review of phonetics, phonemics—words contrasted to highlight sound differences. Wide range of material: talk between family members, friends; sightseeing; adaptation of Tolstoy's "The Shark;" history of Academy of Sciences; proverbs, epigrams; Pushkin, Lermontov, Fet, Blok, Maikov poems. Conversation passages spoken twice, fast and slow, let you anticipate answers, hear all sounds but understand normal speed. 12″ 33⅓ record, album sleeve. 44-page manual with entire record text. Translation on facing pages, phonetic instructions.   The set **$4.95**

Note: For students wishing to use a grammar as well, set is available with grammar-text on which record is based, Gronicka and Bates-Yakobson's "Essentials of Russian" (400pp., 6 x 9, clothbound; Prentice Hall), an excellent, standard text used in scores of colleges, institutions.
                              Augmented set: book, record, manual, sleeve **$10.70**

DICTIONARY OF SPOKEN RUSSIAN, English-Russian, Russian-English. Based on phrases and complete sentences, rather than isolated words; recognized as one of the best methods of learning the idiomatic speech of a country. Over 11,500 entries, indexed by single words, with more than 32,000 English and Russian sentences and phrases, in immediately useable form. Probably the largest list ever published. Shows accent changes in conjugation and declension; irregular forms listed in both alphabetical place and under main form of word. 15,000 word introduction covering Russian sounds, writing, grammar, syntax. 15-page appendix of geographical names, money, important signs, given names, foods, special Soviet terms, etc. Travellers, businessmen, students, government employees have found this their best source for Russian expressions. Originally published as War Department Technical Manual TM 30-944. iv + 573pp. 5⅝ x 8⅜.   T496 Paperbound **$3.00**

THE GIFT OF LANGUAGE, M. Schlauch. Formerly titled THE GIFT OF TONGUES, this is a middle-level survey that avoids both superficiality and pedantry. It covers such topics as linguistic families, word histories, grammatical processes in such foreign languages as Aztec, Ewe, and Bantu, semantics, language taboos, and dozens of other fascinating and important topics. Especially interesting is an analysis of the word-coinings of Joyce, Cummings, Stein and others in terms of linguistics. 232 bibliographic notes. Index. viii + 342pp. 5⅜ x 8.
                              T243 Paperbound **$1.95**

Prices subject to change without notice.

Dover publishes books on art, music, philosophy, literature, languages, history, social sciences, psychology, handcrafts, orientalia, puzzles and entertainments, chess, pets and gardens, books explaining science, intermediate and higher mathematics, mathematical physics, engineering, biological sciences, earth sciences, classics of science, etc. Write to:

Dept. catrr.
Dover Publications, Inc.
180 Varick Street, N. Y. 14, N. Y.